Cooking with Coco

By the same author

Portrait of Pasta
Good Housekeeping Italian Cookery
Pasta Perfect
Gastronomy of Italy
Secrets from an Italian Kitchen
Entertaining All'Italiana
The Classic Food of Northern Italy
Amaretto, Apple Cake and Artichokes
Risotto with Nettles

Cooking with Coco

FAMILY RECIPES TO COOK TOGETHER

Anna Del Conte

photographs by Jason Lowe

Chatto & Windus

LONDON

Published by Chatto & Windus 2011

2 4 6 8 10 9 7 5 3 1

Copyright © Anna Del Conte 2011
Photographs copyright © Jason Lowe 2011

Anna Del Conte has asserted her right under the Copyright, Designs
and Patents Act 1988 to be identified as the author of this work

First published in Great Britain in 2011 by
Chatto & Windus
Random House, 20 Vauxhall Bridge Road,
London SW1V 2SA

www.randomhouse.co.uk

Addresses for companies within The Random House Group Limited can be found at: www.randomhouse.co.uk/offices.htm

The Random House Group Limited Reg. No. 954009

A CIP catalogue record for this book
is available from the British Library

ISBN 9780701184889

The Random House Group Limited supports The Forest Stewardship Council (FSC), the leading international forest certification
organisation. All our titles that are printed on Greenpeace approved FSC certified paper carry the FSC logo. Our paper procurement
policy can be found at: www.randomhouse.co.uk/environment

Design by willwebb.co.uk

Printed and bound in China by
C&C Offset Printing Co., Ltd

For Nell, Johnny, Coco, Kate and Viktor

Introduction

Coco is my 12-year-old granddaughter and my tireless helper in the kitchen. Her ambition in life is to open a restaurant that she will call *'il ristorante della Nonna'*, where she will recreate all the dishes we have cooked together.

Coco liked being in the kitchen from a very early age. I used to sit her down, with a spoon and a piece of bread, or a sprig of parsley and a clove of garlic in front of her, and she would try to copy whatever I was doing. Like any other child, she enjoyed it because she liked being with me and being talked to. And of course I liked it too – a lovely cheerful face smiling at me; far easier for me than playing and also far more productive, since I had to be in the kitchen in any case to prepare a meal. I taught Coco to smell food and I gave her titbits to taste during the different stages of cooking. Soon enough she was able to do the simplest jobs, like arranging decorations on a cake. Her favourite job was weighing out ingredients, which we did with old-fashioned weighing scales. I would put the flour or the sugar in the bowl and she would put the weights on the flat plate – she put the copper weights on or took them off or changed them; and so she also learnt some arithmetic along the way.

When Coco first began to help me she loved to shower grated Parmesan onto a mound of risotto. She would pick up the cheese with her fingers and then try to sprinkle it over; it usually finished up all together in a lump. But she soon enlarged her repertoire and now, after several years by my side in the kitchen, she can make many dishes all on her own – such as custard, biscuits, mousses and some sauces. At the moment she is passionate about Moroccan cooking, thanks to her mother's tantalising descriptions of the delicious food she ate while she was on holiday there. So Coco now forgoes meat pies in favour of tagines, she experiments with kofta and pilaf and couscous, and leaves risotto and pasta aside. Of course we don't just make foreign food; I teach her my Italian dishes but I also want her to learn the English dishes that are part of the culture of her country.

Coco loves shopping, by which I don't just mean buying toys and tops, but also tomatoes and lamb. I have shown her what to look for when we buy fennel bulbs (the bottom and the outside should be creamy and have no brown spots); French beans (they should snap when you bend them and not just floppily bow); beef (it should have a yellowish fat, not spanking white); prosciutto (with a lovely strip of fat around it); Parmesan (its colour and texture), and so on and so forth. She listens and absorbs.

We also talk about the seasons and I have tried to teach her how important they are to good cooking. Unfortunately, in Britain seasons hardly matter any more. You can buy almost anything all year round. Children nowadays, alas, do not have the thrill of eating the first cherries in June and making a wish, as we used to when I was a child in Milan, or the first peaches in July and the first mandarins in November. But I tell my grandchildren that a tomato salad in the middle of January, for instance, is not only tasteless, but also is not in harmony with the weather. A rich risotto of mushrooms is far more enjoyable in the autumn, while one made with fresh vegetables can only be eaten in the spring. Who wants a beef stew or baked lasagne in July? Dishes, like ingredients, have seasons.

My mother used to say that 'a good dish begins in the shop' and I will add that a good chef begins in the shop too. During our time together in the kitchen, I know that Coco has learnt the basics of cooking. She has also learnt the importance of the ingredients you buy, the respect you must have for each of them, and the ability to taste and criticise and improve.

Tasting is a very important part of cooking, yet it is so often overlooked. 'But how do you teach a child the criteria for judging a dish?' How indeed? Well, through experience and discussing with your young helper the merits or otherwise of what you are making. Encourage your Coco to make comments, negative as well as positive, and to try to express the reasons behind those comments. Your taste might be slightly different, but you will soon find out that if she judges that a little more chilli is needed or an extra pinch of salt, you will agree. Just as a child learns how to appreciate paintings by being taken to galleries, or to understand and love music by listening, the same applies with food: frequent exposure to good food and systematic analysis will teach so much.

There is no main course as such in Italian cooking. There are usually two principal courses, which are never brought to the table at the same time. After a pasta, a risotto or a soup, your taste buds get ready for the next dish, which is often a vegetable dish or a fresh salad. I have passed on to my grandchildren the Italian habit of having more than one course in a meal. I agree that one course can be as big as three smaller courses, but it is boring to eat the same thing until you are full. Far more satisfying – and civilised – to have a change. So, in this book, you might find that the quantities are a bit on the mean side, if you want to cook only one dish as a main course. In that case, just increase them, remembering that when you increase the quantity of the main ingredient you don't have to increase the amount of butter or oil in the same proportions. For instance, if the recipe calls for 400g pasta and 6 tablespoons oil but you want to cook 600g pasta, you only need 7 tablespoons oil, not 8. You have also to be more parsimonious with spices and all other strong flavourings.

Also remember that these recipes are to be shared with children – many of them make enough for four people, but I am thinking of gatherings that include little ones. For instance, one egg per child is certainly enough, as is 100g boned chicken.

I find it extremely difficult to give the exact cooking time for some dishes – there are so many factors to take into consideration: the strength of the heat (which may be gas, electricity or induction); the size and thickness of the pan; the size and quality of the ingredients, and so on. After 40 years of professional cooking, I am still learning. No dish is ever the same the second time round – and this, for me, is one of the many appeals of cooking.

The precise cooking time does not matter when the dish in question is something like a casserole, nor when you can taste the dish and decide for yourself. But when frying a piece of meat, or making custard, for example, a minute makes all the difference. My suggestion is to learn to use your eyes, not only to keep an eye on the clock but also to look at the food you're cooking; to use your nose – you can always smell a cake or French beans when they're done, because cooked food always has a stronger smell; and to use your ears, as, for example, when making custard the noise of the wooden spoon against the pan will change as the mixture thickens. And, of course, it also depends on your own preferences. Learn by experience and try to be your own judge. You will see that cooking can never really be an exact science.

Unlike all my previous books, this one contains many recipes for sweet things. You can see why. If you want your young ones to help, you must encourage them into the kitchen with the prospect of eating food they like. And in this way they will happily learn how to cook.

Cooking with Coco is divided into four sections, which move through the different stages as children get older: starting at around age 3, then progressing to age 6, age 9 and finishing on the brink of the teenage years. A few of the recipes that appear in the first section are very simple indeed and they might be repeated later, when they are developed into more complex dishes. All the recipes are based on my own experience – first as a child, and then as a mother and a grandmother. But these sections are simply guidelines. After all, every child is different in their development as well as in their likes and dislikes. And even if I seldom cooked food with the children that was suitable only for them, I always took their tastes into consideration. I never asked Nell, my oldest granddaughter, now 16, to cook a fish, because she doesn't like fish; nor Johnny, her 14-year-old brother, to fry a lamb chop, lamb not being part of his culinary dictionary. I never go into the kitchen with Coco and her siblings just to make treats but I always keep in mind the food that they like best, which naturally is the food they most like to cook, just like any of us. We cook all sorts of food together, although I try to choose recipes that can involve them, like a *puttanesca* for their spaghetti, a sauce which takes only 10 minutes to make and involves a lot of throwing ingredients into the pan (rather than my tomato sauce, which takes 40 minutes and requires no throwing things in).

I enjoyed working on this book very much because I enjoy being with Coco very much. I hope the book will give you pleasure in the kitchen with your children or grandchildren or great-grandchildren.

As I have a Coco, I have used 'she' and 'her' throughout the book. But if you have a Jack or an Oliver in the kitchen, then of course read 'he', 'him' and 'his' instead. The cooking is the same and also, I hope, his enjoyment.

Basic Tips

When I cook with or for children, I prefer to use organic ingredients because I feel strongly that children should have as few chemicals in their diet as possible.

- I buy only organic lemons, because I often use the zest and do not want to grate wax or pesticides into my food.
- I use only large organic eggs, because I often use raw eggs or eggs that are not completely cooked.
- I buy only unsalted butter because I prefer the flavour and I don't want added salt in my food.
- I use sea salt because it is healthier.
- I use Italian 00 flour because, unlike most white flour, it has no additives (they call them 'manufacturing aids'). It is also very finely milled and so more suitable for many dishes.
- I buy farm-raised chicken because, amongst other considerations, it has a far superior flavour.
- I never buy meat in supermarkets because of the pressure put on suppliers to produce cheap food in large quantities.

To sum up, I buy the best-quality food available for two reasons: first, because it is generally superior in flavour and, second, because I believe it is better for my grandchildren's health.

Breadcrumbs

In this book, you will find quite a few recipes containing breadcrumbs. Of course you can buy them, but the ones you make yourself will be better and you have the reassurance of knowing what they're made of. It's also a very good use of bread which otherwise would be thrown away. Use only good-quality white bread, although a mixture of white and wholemeal may be all right, as long as the brown bread does not contain seeds. Brown bread has a more pronounced flavour that might interfere with the flavour of the dish you are making. The bread should have a coarse texture, like a *pain rustique*.

For dried breadcrumbs, remove the crust and break the bread into small pieces. Spread them out on a baking tray and place the tray in a warm oven. I usually put the tray in just after I have turned the oven off. The oven is hot enough to toast the bread, and it doesn't matter if you forget about it; it will not burn. When ready, blitz the bread in a food processor to very fine crumbs. I store breadcrumbs in a jar in the fridge, where they keep for about one month. Or you can keep them for longer in the freezer.

To make fresh breadcrumbs, use good-quality white bread that is one or two days old. Remove the crustiest part of the crust and break the bread into pieces. Put the pieces in the food processor and blitz to fine crumbs. Spread the crumbs out on a tray and let them dry for a few hours, before storing them in the fridge, or in the freezer if you have made a lot (there is no need to defrost them before using). You can also buy good fresh breadcrumbs in supermarkets.

Pasta

I am sure you know how to cook pasta, but may I remind you of a few steps that are essential for cooking pasta well.

Use a large pot. A pasta pot should be tall and narrow, like a top hat. The general rule for the amount of water needed is 1 litre water to 100g pasta. The salt should be crystal sea salt added in the proportion of 1 dessertspoon (10g) salt to 1 litre of water. This might seem a lot of salt to you, but please remember that the water in which the pasta cooks is not absorbed by the pasta. The water should be boiling fast before the pasta is added and the pasta should cook over a high heat. The length of cooking depends on the quality and the shape of the pasta. My advice is to taste 1 minute before the end of the given time in the manufacturer's instructions.

Pasta should be drained as soon as it is ready. Do not over-drain it; it should be slippery. Tip the pasta into a large colander and give the colander two sharp shakes. Immediately turn the pasta into a heated bowl or back into the saucepan and mix in the sauce. It is far easier to dress pasta in a big container than on individual plates. If the sauce is not ready, mix 2 tablespoons of oil into the pasta. Do not leave undressed pasta standing.

And tell your children to start eating as soon as it is on their plates. 'Pasta should not wait for anybody', as we say in Italy.

1
Mixing
& Messing

This is exactly what I expected Coco to do with her little chubby hands when, at the age of 2 or 3, she started coming into the kitchen to 'help you cooking'.

She loved to chop with the mezzaluna – half-moon – which is a safe knife, since both small hands are occupied on the handles. (Although it goes without saying that you must supervise carefully at all times.) Other favourite activities were cutting biscuits into different shapes, however unsuccessfully; pushing a pea into a fried risotto ball or a bit of mozzarella into a meat rissole; and patting breadcrumbs onto a veal chop or onto a slice of aubergine. She was as happy to be with me as I was happy to be with her, keeping an eye on her while I got on with the task at hand. A perfect arrangement.

Minestrina *A light soup*

Not long ago, my daughter Julia, without whom this book would never have materialised, was going through my list of recipes and called out: 'But, Mummy, you haven't included *minestrina*. They all loved it, don't you remember?' Yes, of course I remember, just as I remember liking it so very much when I was a child.

Minestrina is the comfort food par excellence of many Northern Italians and, even more so, it is the panacea for all the ills of their children. The child is sick, give him *minestrina* to nourish him; the child is overexcited, give him *minestrina* to quieten him down; the child is bad-tempered, *minestrina* will soothe him; the child doesn't want to swallow anything, he will swallow a spoonful or two of *minestrina*. Certainly this was my mantra with my own children.

But what is this miracle food? It is just stock – good, light stock – in which small pasta shapes (*pastina* in Italian) are boiled. The most common shapes are: *stelline* (little stars – Coco's favourite); *orzo* (barley); *alfabeto* (alphabet); *avemarie* (holy Mary); *anellini* (little rings); *semini* (little seeds).

Minestrina should be made with the best stock: meat or chicken for added nourishment; vegetable for easier digestion. Having said that, you can make a very good *minestrina* even if you don't have any home-made stock in your fridge or freezer; just use a good, shop-bought organic chicken, beef or vegetable stock powder or concentrate (I use Marigold Swiss vegetable bouillon powder).

Serves 4

1.25 litres stock
　　(see recipe p.20)
125g *pastina*
freshly grated Parmigiano-
　　Reggiano, to serve

Bring the stock to the boil, add the *pastina* and stir until the stock comes back to the boil. Turn the heat down to low and cook according to the directions on the pasta packet. The method for cooking pasta in a soup differs slightly from that for cooking pasta to be eaten *asciutta* – drained. The stock must boil gently and the pan should be partly covered with a lid. I put the lid askew on the pan. This is to prevent the *pastina* from sticking to the bottom of the pan and the stock from evaporating. Also, *pastina* in a stock should be slightly more cooked than pasta *asciutta*.

Stir the soup occasionally and taste near the end of cooking. The pasta might need a minute or two more. Serve the soup, and hand round the Parmesan.

The Stock

If I make stock I make this classic Italian one with beef as well as chicken, but never with lamb or pork. But, if you have a favourite recipe for chicken stock, use that. Remember that the meat or chicken used to make stock is good later in a rice or pasta salad, in a curry, served with salsa verde, used in meatballs, or sautéed in an onion sauce.

Makes 1.5–2 litres

1.5kg assorted meat and
    chicken wings
marrow bones or other
    beef bones
1 onion, cut in half and stuck
    with 2 cloves
2 carrots, cut into chunks
2 celery stalks, cut into chunks
1 leek, cut into chunks
1 ripe tomato, cut in half
a few parsley stalks
2 bay leaves
3 litres cold water
sea salt, to taste

Put the meat, bones, vegetables and herbs in a stockpot, then add the 3 litres of cold water – or enough to cover – and bring to the boil. The water must be cold to begin with so that the meat and the vegetables can slowly release their juices. Set the lid very slightly askew on the pot, to let some of the steam escape. Turn the heat down to the minimum for the stock to simmer. After a few minutes, remove the scum which comes to the surface with a slotted spoon and then cook the stock for about 3 hours. Strain and, when cold, refrigerate it.

Remove the fat that has solidified on the surface. At the end of the operation, there still might be a few specks of fat that are hard to remove. Heat the stock and lay a piece of kitchen paper on the surface for a moment. As you lift the paper off again the fatty bits will stick to it.

Now taste and, if you think the stock is rather mild, reduce it over a high heat. Then season with salt, cover with clingfilm and, when cold, put in the fridge.

The stock for a *minestrina* should be clarified, but this is a book of recipes to make with the children, and, quite frankly, I don't think your Coco will mind if the stock is not clear and limpid.

Il tricolore sul piatto

Mozzarella, tomato and basil salad

This is one of the first things – hardly a recipe – I made with Coco, and before that with my own children whom I made sure were far more knowledgeable about my origins. They loved to make an Italian flag with this salad and then eat it up. It is a very visual dish. Coco used to place the basil leaves over the tomatoes. As soon as I knew she could handle a knife, she learnt to peel the tomatoes and to cut the mozzarella into small cubes, sometimes with less than perfect results. If we didn't have basil, I gave her strips of lettuce to place in a criss-cross fashion over the tomatoes.

Serves 4, as a starter
8 large ripe tomatoes
350g buffalo mozzarella
5 tbsp extra-virgin olive oil
16 basil leaves
sea salt and freshly ground
    black pepper, to taste

Make a tiny cross at the bottom of each tomato. Bring a pan of water to the boil and plunge in the tomatoes. Count to 30, then drain the tomatoes and put them in a bowl of cold water.

With little fingers or a small knife peel off the skin, which, if the tomatoes are properly ripe, will come away quite easily. Cut the tomatoes in half along their 'equator' and squeeze out a little of the seeds and juice. Sprinkle the inside of each tomato with a little salt and lay them, cut side down, on a wooden board. Place the tomatoes in the fridge for half an hour to firm up. It does not matter if you leave them longer.

Then gently wipe the inside of the tomatoes with kitchen paper and place 2 of them on each plate. Coco and I use dessert plates, a little smaller than dinner plates in which the 2 halves of the tomatoes would look lost.

Cut the mozzarella into small chunks and divide these into 16 mounds. Put a mound into each tomato half and sprinkle with pepper. (Coco loved pepper from an early age.) Drizzle with the oil and place a basil leaf over each half.

Prosciutto and melon

Prosciutto is a favourite of most children and so is melon. I started presenting them in a more interesting way than the usual slices for Coco when she was very young. We used to make this antipasto both with grissini (see p.218) and with melon. Coco still does this when she has friends for tea.

I find melons the most difficult fruit to buy. I can never tell how good they are. You cannot judge by the weight, the smell, the hardness, the softness. But what I do find is that they taste better if I leave them for 2 or 3 days to ripen in the house, not the fridge, before I use them. My favourite melons are cantaloupes, but they aren't easily available – so you could buy the more common galia and hope it is good.

Serves 4

1 melon

250g prosciutto

Cut the melon into quarters, remove the seeds and cut away the skin. Cut each quarter into thin wedges of about 2cm. Cut the slices of prosciutto in half lengthwise, lay the halves in front of your Coco and show her how to wrap a piece round one end of each melon wedge. That's it. But most children like this slippery job and they usually like eating the end result.

Broad bean
and goat's cheese salad

Coco loved to pod broad beans when she was little, but even more she loved to skin them when cooked. She would get hold of a bean between her thumb and forefinger and squeeze, and the bean popped out 'all naked' as she would say.

Serves 4

1.5kg broad beans,
    weight before podding
150g fresh goat's cheese
6 tbsp extra-virgin olive oil
2 tbsp lemon juice
1 garlic clove, crushed
sea salt and freshly ground
    black pepper, to taste
a few marjoram leaves,
    for sprinkling (optional)

Pod the beans and cook them in plenty of boiling salted water until tender, about 3 minutes. Drain and let them cool enough to be able to handle. Meanwhile cut the goat's cheese into small cubes.

When the beans are no longer too hot, skin them and put them in a bowl. Dress them with 3 tablespoons of the oil while they are still warm, because they can then absorb more oil. Add the lemon juice and the crushed garlic and mix gently with a fork, which is less likely to break the beans. When the beans are cool, add the cheese, the remaining oil and some black pepper. Mix again and taste to check the seasoning. Sprinkle with the marjoram, if you like.

Bresaola with rocket
and Parmesan

The pleasure of making this little antipasto with Coco was to see her face greedily following my hands as I flaked the Parmesan with my vegetable peeler. Every now and then I gave her a flake and when everything was ready we assembled the dish together, or sort of together.

I prefer to use the kind of Parmesan called *Padano* here, as it has a less pronounced flavour which combines better with the bresaola.

To be honest, Coco was not at all keen on eating this dish, Parmesan aside, but she enjoyed making it and I enjoyed eating it. Maybe you'll be lucky and your Coco will like both.

Serves 4
150g rocket or frisée lettuce
2 tbsp extra-virgin olive oil
2 tbsp lemon juice
300g bresaola
75g Parmigiano-Reggiano or
    Grana Padano
freshly ground black pepper,
    to taste

Rinse the rocket (or frisée lettuce), dry it gently and put it in a bowl. Toss with half the olive oil and the lemon juice – you might find that you want a bit less than 2 tablespoons juice. Lay the salad on a dish. Now it is your Coco's job to arrange the bresaola slices. She might like to roll each slice and put it alongside the rocket, or to lay a slice in a soft, undulating pattern over the little mounds of greenery. Shave the cheese with a vegetable peeler and let the wavy flakes fall directly on to the bresaola – a job for Coco. Top the mound with a grinding of black pepper and drizzle the remaining oil over everything.

I coniglietti italiani

Italian rabbits

This is the curious name my children gave to this simple snack that they loved to make and eat when they were young, because of its colour – the colours of the Italian flag. In those days, we had to go all the way to Soho to buy the ricotta and to get a better quality of olive oil than was available locally in Kensington. Decades later, when I started making this with my grandchildren, I didn't have to drive to Soho; any supermarket will stock olive oil and ricotta now, albeit not as good.

I am not going to give the quantities for this snack. It all depends on how much you want to make, but here is what we have always done.

I buy some small plum or cherry tomatoes, a pot of ricotta, and some French beans which I steam until al dente. Then I cut the top off each tomato and scoop out seeds and pulp with the pointed handle of a teaspoon. I sprinkle the inside of the tomatoes with a little salt, place them upside down on a board and put the board in the fridge for an hour or so. When the time is up, I spoon 2 or 3 tablespoons of ricotta into a bowl, pour in I or 2 tablespoons of best olive oil, season it with salt and a little pepper and mix well with a fork. Then I call Coco, give her a piece of kitchen paper and show her how to dry the tomatoes inside and out. With a small teaspoon I help her to fill each tomato with some of the ricotta. And then we cut each bean into lengths of about 3cm and she sticks 2 beans into the ricotta: the ears of the rabbit. The result is great fun to look at and very pleasing in its clean and fresh taste.

Crumpet pizzas

When I first came to England, some 60 years ago, there was one thing I could not resist when I went to the baker's on the Fulham Road to buy bread: crumpets. I often bought only one, a solitary crumpet that I ate hot and dripping with butter for tea. It was the only time I found that salted butter was just right. If I used unsalted butter, I would have to add a pinch of salt. I love my crumpets savoury. So, years later when I read a recipe for 'Crumpet Pizza' in Book Two of Delia Smith's *How to Cook* series, I immediately tried it and have made these easy *pizze* ever since. Delia gives the recipe for a Gorgonzola and mozzarella topping – delicious – but, as she says, 'you can get really creative and make up loads more ideas of your own'. In fact, you can top the crumpets with any of the *pizzelle* toppings on p.34. And that is what I used to do with Coco when I didn't have time or couldn't be bothered to make *pizzelle*.

Serves 4

4 crumpets
175g Gorgonzola, cubed
50g mozzarella, cubed
50g chopped walnuts
8 medium sage leaves
extra-virgin olive oil,
    for brushing

We grill the crumpets under a low heat until they are just golden on both sides and then we place them on a baking tray. Coco mixes together the cheeses and the walnuts and then divides the mixture into 4 mounds and places a mound on each crumpet. She brushes each sage leaf with a little olive oil and she places 2 leaves over each mound. We turn the grill up to high and place the tray under the grill, but not too close to the heat. In 4–5 minutes the crumpet pizzas, dripping with melted cheeses, are ready to be shoved into greedy little mouths.

Pizzelle

Fried pizzas

When I was a child, we never cooked pizza at home. Pizza was something we ate at the pizzeria when we were on holiday. As a consequence, I never made pizza with my children, nor, as a matter of fact, do I make it now with my grandchildren. And I know that, in Italy, very few people make pizza at home, because you cannot make a real pizza in a domestic oven.

What my mother used to make, to our greatest delight, were *pizzelle*, small fried *pizze* with classic pizza toppings like margherita or marinara.

Pizzelle were favourites of my children and they are now favourites of Coco and her siblings.

We prepare 3 or 4 toppings so there is an exciting choice. The usual toppings are: tomato sauce plus another ingredient that Coco fancies (see p.34), or ham and mushroom (p.34) and no tomato, or a delicious onion marmalade with anchovy fillets (p.35). Of course your Coco might like pineapple and ham, as mine does, but frankly the thought of pineapple on pizza makes me feel sick. So if Coco wants a pizza with pineapple and ham, she'll have to make it without me.

Makes about 10–12 *pizzelle*
For the pizzelle *bases:*
200g Italian 00 flour
½ tsp dried yeast
1 tsp sea salt
1 tbsp olive oil, plus more
    for greasing
100–200ml warm water
vegetable oil, for frying

First make the dough and then, while the dough is resting, you can make the topping. Like all Italians, I make the dough directly on the work surface not in a bowl, simply because there is one less thing to wash up at the end. But you can do whatever you are used to.

Shape the flour into a mound and mix in the yeast and the salt. Then make a well in the centre of your mound, into which you pour the 1 tablespoon olive oil and about 100ml warm water. Begin to knead the dough by gathering flour from the sides of the well and into the middle. Add more water until the dough sticks together. Knead by pressing and pushing the dough away from you for about 7 minutes and then form it into a ball. Grease a bowl with a little oil and place the dough into it. Turn the ball so that it is oiled all over. Cover with a thick tea towel and leave to rise in a warm corner of the kitchen for 2 or 3 hours, until it has doubled in size.

While the dough is resting, make the topping of your choice (pp.34 and 35).

When the dough is more or less double its original volume, knock it back by punching the air out of it with your fist and stretch and roll it out into a thickness of about 3mm. This is something any child likes to do, although it is not easy to roll out pizza dough because it wants to spring back. But eventually you will win.

Get a biscuit cutter of about 8cm diameter and stamp out as many discs as you can. Knead the leftover scraps of dough and cut out more discs until you have used all the dough.

Preheat the oven to 200°C/gas mark 6.

Pour the vegetable oil into a wok or a frying pan to a depth of 1cm and fry the *pizzelle* until golden, about 2 minutes on each side. This is categorically not Coco's work, not even now that she is 12. Boiling oil terrifies me, as indeed it should. But I let Coco stand and watch what happens. Frying is a fascinating method of cooking, but a difficult one, and children learn a lot by watching and recording what happens to the food. You may need to fry in several batches, depending on the size of your pan, adding more oil with each new batch. Lay the fried *pizzelle* on kitchen paper to soak up the excess oil.

When all the *pizzelle* are fried, the fun starts for the children as they can now top them with whatever they choose. Put the topped *pizzelle* on a baking tray and bake them in the oven for 4 or 5 minutes.

A tomato sauce

I have often tried to make tomato sauce, both for pizza or pasta, with fresh tomatoes: cherry, plum, British local, big, small, red or yellow; but I find that the best tomato sauce is made with tinned San Marzano tomatoes. I have also tried to roast the fresh tomatoes before making the sauce so as to concentrate the flavour. Again, I didn't get the result that I wanted. As all Italian cooks know, tomato sauce is best made with tinned tomatoes – full stop, end of story. So here is the recipe for the tomato sauce we make for *pizzelle*.

400g tin chopped tomatoes
1 garlic clove, crushed
2 tbsp extra-virgin olive oil
sea salt, to taste

Put the tinned tomatoes, garlic, oil and salt into a saucepan, bring to the boil and cook for some 30 minutes over a lively heat, until the sauce is thick. Stir occasionally.

Now Coco comes into action, first by testing and checking the seasoning then by spreading a little sauce on the *pizzelle*, and then by adding whatever ingredients she fancies. These are the ones I usually put on the table: a sliced buffalo mozzarella; grated mature Cheddar; a dozen leaves of fresh basil; 1–2 teaspoons dried oregano; some grated Parmesan; a few slices of a small chorizo or salami; 3 or 4 anchovy fillets; and, sometimes, a tin of tuna. All these ingredients go very well on a tomato topping.

For the ham and mushroom topping:

2 tbsp extra-virgin olive oil
1 garlic clove, crushed
100g chestnut mushrooms,
    sliced
grating of nutmeg (optional)
120g ham, cut into matchsticks
3 tbsp freshly grated
    Parmigiano-Reggiano
sea salt and freshly ground
    black pepper, to taste

Heat the oil in a small frying pan with the garlic and as soon as the garlic begins to colour throw in the mushrooms and cook over a high heat until the oil has been absorbed, stirring the whole time. Add the nutmeg (if using) and salt and pepper to taste, then lower the heat and continue cooking for a further 5–7 minutes, stirring occasionally. Add the ham and the cheese and mix well. At this point I give a spoon to Coco so that she can check the seasoning.

For the onion and anchovy fillets topping:

500g sweet onions, finely sliced
4 tsp olive oil
1 tsp granulated sugar
1 garlic clove, finely chopped
4 salted anchovies, cleaned, or
    8 anchovy fillets, chopped
sea salt and freshly ground
    black pepper, to taste

Put the onion, oil, sugar, garlic and a little salt in a sauté pan and cook, covered, for about 45 minutes over a low heat, turning the onion over and over occasionally. Don't be tempted to turn the heat up so that the onion will cook quicker. The sauce will not be good. Add a couple of tablespoons of hot water whenever the sauce becomes too dry. The onion should not fry, just stew. Add the anchovies and some black pepper and continue cooking at the lowest simmer for 4 or 5 minutes, pressing the anchovies down to mash them.

Bruschetta

This is the traditional bruschetta of Rome and Tuscany, made with those incredible tasty local tomatoes. Coco loves to make it, especially at the family home in Le Marche, in Italy, where we always make it outside on the barbecue. But you can also make bruschetta on a domestic grill. It's the ideal summer snack as part of an antipasto with salami and prosciutto.

Serves 4

5–6 ripe tomatoes

1 ciabatta

6 tbsp extra-virgin olive oil

2 garlic cloves, cut in half

sea salt and freshly ground
    black pepper, to taste

handful of basil leaves,
    to garnish

Cut the tomatoes into small pieces, discarding the core. Put into a bowl and sprinkle with salt. The salt will bring out the flavour.

Cut the ciabatta diagonally into slices, about 1cm thick. Score each slice lightly with the point of a knife and place on the barbecue rack. Moisten with olive oil and then grill until charred on both sides. While they are still hot, rub with the garlic.

Now pick up the tomato pieces with a teaspoon and place them on the grilled bread. Season with black pepper and dress with a few drops of olive oil. Place a basil leaf over each slice – and enjoy.

Stuffed mussels

Even I was surprised to see Coco's joy when, aged something like 2, a mountain of mussels was set before her at the restaurant on the beach where we had driven from the house in Le Marche to spend the day at the sea. She laughed and screamed and waved her arms around and greedily sucked the juice from the shells. I remember all the people around our table laughing and then asking us about the chubby little girl who obviously adored mussels. Even in Italy she was an oddity.

I started making this dish with her sometime around then. She used to sit in her high chair at the kitchen table and, while I was stuffing one mussel, she would quickly sneak another into her mouth. In between, she tried to help me to stuff the others.

Serves 4–6

1.5kg mussels
1 organic lemon
150g dried white breadcrumbs
   (see p.12)
2 garlic cloves, finely chopped
pinch or 2 dried crushed chilli
120g flat-leaf parsley, chopped
100ml extra-virgin olive oil
4 tbsp grated pecorino cheese
sea salt, to taste (optional)

Preheat the oven to 200°C/gas mark 6.

To clean the mussels, throw them into a sink full of cold water and scrub them with a hard brush, scraping off any barnacles with a small knife and pulling off the beards. Discard any mussels that are not closed and do not close when you tap them on a hard surface. Change the water and rinse again until the water in the sink remains clean.

Cut the lemon into wedges and put them in a large frying pan. Add the mussels and put the pan, covered with a lid, on a high heat. Shake the pan occasionally so that all the mussels come into contact with the hot bottom of the pan. When the mussels are open – this will take about 4 minutes – take off the heat and chuck away any mussels that are still closed and also one half of each shell.

Now that the mussels are ready, prepare the stuffing. First strain the liquid left at the bottom of the pan. Sometimes this is clear, but sometimes you can see some sediment at the bottom. If so, pour the liquid gently through a sieve lined with a piece of muslin. Whatever you do, do it slowly so that, if there is a grain or two of sand, it will stay at the bottom of the pan. Then put the breadcrumbs, garlic, chilli and parsley into a bowl and mix well. Add about 4 or 5 tablespoons of the mussel liquid and nearly all the oil, leaving behind just 1 or 2 tablespoons. Mix again – little hands are helpful here – taste, and check the seasoning. Usually you don't need to add any salt.

Place the mussels in their half shells on 2 baking trays. With your fingers, pick up a good pinch of the crumb mixture and press it down onto each mussel, covering it well and filling the shell. Sprinkle them all with the pecorino and drizzle with the remaining oil.

Bake for 10 minutes until the crumbs have formed a crust at the top. Coco eats them hot or cold, or indeed at any temperature. I prefer them lukewarm. *Squisito.*

Hard-boiled eggs
with breadcrumbs and parsley topping

There is absolutely nothing to this dish – apart from the fact that Coco liked making it from a very tender age. I confess I cannot remember how much she liked to *eat* it, but I did. It is very good.

Serves 4

6 hard-boiled eggs
5 tbsp extra-virgin olive oil
1 tbsp cider vinegar
½ small fresh chilli, seeded and
    chopped
3 tbsp chopped flat-leaf parsley
1 garlic clove, chopped
4 tbsp fresh breadcrumbs,
    white or brown (see p.13)
pinch of sea salt, or to taste
12 black or green olives

I like the yolks of my hard-boiled eggs just set, not rubbery and turning green, and this is how you do it: bring a saucepan of water to the boil and then gently lower the eggs into the water with a spoon. When the water comes back to the boil, turn the heat down so that the water just simmers and cook the eggs for 7 minutes. After that, put the pan under cold running water and as soon as you can handle the eggs, peel them and cut them in half lengthwise.

Next prepare the topping. Heat the oil and vinegar in a small frying pan, mix in the chilli, parsley, garlic and breadcrumbs and fry for 3–4 minutes. Add a pinch of salt and now ask your Coco to help you with the final stage. Pile about 2 teaspoons of the mixture over each half egg and press down gently. My Coco loved doing this – and then sticking an olive on the top of each half egg.

Ruote, chicken, ham
and pea salad

I am not very keen on cold pasta or coloured pasta. But all my grandchildren are and sometimes I submit. Coloured pasta is a gimmick, but it is attractive, I must admit. And here it is served as a salad, a modern creation. Pasta salads are difficult to make well; often the result is a thick and gooey mess. However, cold pasta dishes are more fun to make with children, because they can choose their own ingredients to be added once the pasta is cooked. For this recipe below, for instance, I sometimes put out Gruyère, cut into small cubes, which can be added as well or used to replace the chicken or the ham. It's a treat for Coco when I prepare a few mushrooms, just quickly sautéed in a little oil. She adores mushrooms and they combine very well with the other ingredients.

This is a dish that I based on the rice salad of my childhood by simply changing the main ingredient. It is ideal for using up that little bit of roast chicken left from Sunday lunch.

If you cannot find coloured *ruote* (wheels), use plain ones or coloured fusilli or another shape of short pasta, but not spaghetti or other long-strand shapes.

Serves 4–6
300g coloured *ruote*
5 tbsp mild extra-virgin olive oil
150g cooked chicken, cut into
    small cubes
100g ham, thickly sliced and
    cut into short strips
100g cooked peas
½ tbsp cider vinegar
1 tsp French mustard
sea salt and freshly ground
    black pepper, to taste
small bunch of chives,
    to garnish

Cook the pasta in plenty of salted boiling water and drain when slightly undercooked. Cold pasta needs to be even more al dente than pasta served hot. Refresh immediately under cold water and pat dry with kitchen paper. Turn the pasta out into a bowl and toss with 1 tablespoon of the oil. Leave it until cold.

Mix in the chicken, ham and peas. Put the vinegar, mustard and the remaining oil into a separate small bowl and beat. Add to the pasta, together with the pepper, and mix thoroughly with a fork. Taste and check the seasoning and then snip the chives all over the top. (If your Coco doesn't like chives, use parsley – the safest of all herbs – instead.)

Meatballs

I started making *polpette* with Coco when she was very young, partly because I remembered how much I loved making them with our cook, Maria, when I was a girl. I hoped to pass on to Coco my enthusiasm for this simple dish, which can also be transformed into something truly luxurious, as Maria did in the autumn when she put small bits of white truffle – my favourite treat – into each meatball. (Something not many of us can afford to do these days!)

When she was very little, Coco simply mixed and mixed the meat with whichever ingredient I chose to put in – a lovely messy job. But as she grew older, I provided different ingredients for her to choose from: parsley or oregano, Gruyère or mozzarella, Parmesan or Cheddar, mortadella or prosciutto, garlic or onion or both, all chopped up and ready for the mix. She decided which ones to add and then moulded the meatballs into golf-ball size, tennis-ball size, walnut-size, squashed hemispheres, or egg shapes. At the end there was the choice of the sauce, if any, to go with them. My grandchildren all have their own favourite sauce so now they take turns to choose which one we should make.

We make meatballs not only with raw meat but also with leftover meat. Personally I cannot bear to go for days on end eating up a roasted joint or roast chicken. I always try to use the leftovers in some interesting way and meatballs are one of the best options.

Meatballs are a blessing at Christmas, perfect for finishing off the never-ending turkey or the ham. A small amount of thick béchamel sauce goes well with minced turkey or minced ham, especially if you add a teaspoon of truffle paste, and a handful or two of chopped sautéed mushrooms. At Easter we mix the minced roast lamb with pounded cumin seeds and a handful of soaked couscous, and so on. Whatever I am doing, I always try to follow the preference of one child or another – the recipes that follow are some of their favourites.

My polpette

These are my favourite *polpette*, which my mother called 'the steak of the poor people'. And indeed they do taste like steak as long as you use good mince. By this, I mean mince that you buy from your butcher who has made it with some chuck steak or shin without any added fat. Beef that you buy already minced does not have that meaty, beefy flavour which is indeed the pleasure of this simple dish.

These meatballs are best with a rich, thick tomato sauce that you can dollop on the side for your Coco to dip each mouthful in. I am ashamed to say that my Coco sometimes puts tomato ketchup on her plate in preference to my tomato sauce (p.34).

Serves 4
500g best lean mince
1 tsp salt
3 tbsp chopped flat-leaf parsley
1 garlic clove, very finely
    chopped or pressed
freshly ground black pepper,
    to taste
2 tbsp olive oil, for frying

In a bowl mix together all the ingredients, except for the oil. Small clean hands are the ideal tools. Pick up about a quarter of the mixture and shape it into a round of about 6–7cm. Press this between your hands to try to eliminate all air pockets and then flatten the ball down to a thickness of about 3cm. Repeat this with the rest of the mixture, to make 4 balls in total. It is far easier to shape meatballs by keeping your hands, or your Coco's hands, moist. These meatballs are best shaped as hamburgers. If you have time, put them in the fridge for at least half an hour before using. This makes them less likely to break up when they cook.

Heat the oil in a non-stick frying pan into which the meatballs will fit comfortably. When the oil is hot, slide the meatballs in and fry them until a dark crust has formed on the bottom (about 2 minutes). Then turn them over and fry the other side for a further 2 minutes. You will see some drops of blood appearing on the surface. It is time to turn down the heat and cook on a gentler heat for another couple of minutes, turning the meatballs over again halfway through. The inside should now be bright pink – and this is the way we like our *polpette*. But if you want your beef more cooked, fry for a further minute, still on a low heat.

Variations

To make Neapolitan meatballs, substitute 2 teaspoons dried oregano for the parsley and mix in 1 buffalo mozzarella, cut into small pieces, and 1 slightly beaten egg. Cook these meatballs for longer, some 9–12 minutes in all.

If we are making meatballs with minced lamb instead of beef, Coco, now that she is 12, likes to add a small tablespoon of harissa to the tomato sauce, because of her passion for Moroccan food.

In the summer we tend to make meatballs the size of walnuts. To the minced meat – beef or pork, or a combination of the two – we add 2 eggs, lots of chopped parsley, 1 or 2 garlic cloves, finely chopped, and 3 or 4 tablespoons grated Parmesan. I like to serve these cold with salsa verde (see below).

Nell's meatballs

My eldest granddaughter, Nell, now aged 16, loves her meatballs finished in this sweet-and-sour sauce. She makes walnut-sized meatballs, which she fries quickly for 2–3 minutes and then puts them in a sauté pan containing 2 tablespoons olive oil, 2 tablespoons wine vinegar, 4 tablespoons water and 2 teaspoons sugar that she has previously brought to the boil. She cooks the meatballs very slowly in this sweet-and-sour sauce for about 5 minutes, turning them over gently halfway through cooking, and then she scatters over them 1 tablespoon sultanas, plumped up by a 20-minute soaking in hot water, and 2 tablespoons pine nuts, which she has previously dry-toasted in a cast-iron pan to bring out the flavour.

Salsa verde for cold polpette (or other cold meat)

3 anchovy fillets
1 garlic clove
3 tbsp flat-leaf parsley
2 tbsp white wine vinegar
4 tbsp extra-virgin olive oil
1 tbsp capers, rinsed and dried
sea salt and freshly ground
    black pepper, to taste

Chop together the anchovy fillets, garlic and parsley. Put them all in a bowl and add the vinegar. Now slowly pour in the oil while beating the whole time with a fork to incorporate the oil. Spoon in the capers, season to taste and pour the sauce over your fried but now cold meatballs. Leave for an hour or so to infuse before serving.

Roasted pepper sauce

This is quite a sophisticated sauce that does not sound like children's food. But I have always made all sorts of food with my children and grandchildren, because I strongly believe that children must learn to eat – and to make – everything, not just fairy cakes and brownies. Coco has learnt to like this sauce, thanks to her brother Johnny who loves palate-scorching food. He begs me to make it so often that Coco has begun to enjoy it too. They both like it with meatballs and Coco also likes it with grilled herrings or mackerel. They peel the peppers and I let them add the capers and anchovies, but I supervise the chilli, because left to his own devices Johnny would be too enthusiastic with it.

Serves 6
1 yellow pepper
1 red pepper
1 green pepper
½ fresh red chilli, seeded and chopped
1 garlic clove
bunch of flat-leaf parsley
3 anchovy fillets, drained
1 tbsp capers, rinsed
4 tbsp extra-virgin olive oil
½ tbsp balsamic vinegar
sea salt, to taste (optional)

Put the whole peppers under the grill and cook them all over, turning them frequently so that the skin is charred but not burnt through. When this is done, put them in a bowl and cover the bowl with clingfilm. Leave for 15 minutes, or longer if you want.

Now remove the skin with a small sharp knife and wipe them clean with kitchen paper. Do not wash them because you will wash away also the lovely burnt juices. When all the peppers are peeled, cut them into quarters and remove and discard the seeds and the white ribs. Cut the peppers into small pieces and put them in a food processor. Add the chilli, garlic, parsley, anchovy fillets and capers. Whiz while you add the oil slowly through the funnel. When the mixture looks smooth, add the balsamic vinegar and taste. Let your Coco decide if she wants to add a bit more of this or of that. The sauce might need a little salt, but usually the capers and the anchovies provide enough saltiness.

Sea bass stuffed with couscous, parsley, fennel and garlic

I put this fish recipe in this section not because Coco could actually make it when she was so young, but because I introduced her – as I did with my own children – to handling fish as early as I could. I wanted them to be familiar with fish, touch it, see inside it, run their hands on the lovely shiny skin and to smell it.

For this dish Coco used to help me by dipping her little hands in the mixture and messing about, and then trying to fill the cavity of the fish. If your fishmonger has not scaled the fish, do not bother to do it yourself. It is a difficult and messy job; you would have scales all over the kitchen. Just cook it as it is and remove the skin before you serve it. But if it's not scaled, don't give it to your Coco to touch: it feels rather unpleasant and it could scratch a child's hands.

Serves 4

1 sea bass, about 1–1.2kg
2 tbsp couscous
2 garlic cloves, chopped
bunch of flat-leaf parsley,
    chopped
2 sprigs wild fennel or 1 tsp
    fennel seeds
4 tbsp mild extra-virgin olive oil
sea salt and freshly ground
    black pepper, to taste
extra-virgin olive oil and lemon
    juice, to serve

Wash the fish inside and out and dry it with kitchen paper.

Put the couscous in a bowl and pour over enough boiling water to cover it. Add the chopped garlic, parsley, fennel, 2 tablespoons of the oil and a little salt and pepper. Leave it to cool a little and now your Coco can come into action by mixing everything together thoroughly with her chubby hands. Put the couscous aside to soak for 20 minutes.

Preheat the oven to 200°C/gas mark 6.

Sprinkle the cavity of the fish with some salt and then, with a teaspoon, fill it with the soaked couscous. Do not overfill or it will spill out during the cooking. Close the opening with a cocktail stick. Line a baking tray with foil, brush with some of the remaining oil and then lay the fish over it. Pour over the last drops of oil and put the tray in the oven. The fish should be cooked in 25–30 minutes. Test it by inserting a knife in the thickest part near the bone. The flesh should come away easily from the bone, but should still be firm.

When the fish is ready, gently pull the skin off the

upper side of the fish, an easy job. Slide a knife down the length of the backbone and flip the top half over. Remove the bone, which will come off quite easily. Turn the bottom half of the fish over on top of the skinned half, and remove the skin. I like to leave the tail and head on because I prefer to present a fish in its entire beauty. Then I slice the fish downwards and place a slice on each plate with a little stuffing on the side. Sprinkle with olive oil and lemon juice and serve.

When a fish is good it does not need any interfering sauce, but if you like you can pass around the Salsa verde for cold polpette (p.45), made with lemon juice instead of vinegar.

Coco's first biscuits

When Coco was very young I made the pastry, rolled it out and then put it in front of her with all the different-shaped cutters we had: dogs, pigs, elephants, stars, hearts – whatever. She was in heaven for an hour or so, while I could get on with cooking something else knowing that she was occupied and happy.

For the flavouring you can use the grated rind of 1 organic lemon, or ½ teaspoon vanilla extract, or ½ teaspoon ground cinnamon, or ½ teaspoon ground ginger, whatever your Coco prefers. My Coco always chose vanilla, while I tried to persuade her that lemon was better, simply because I prefer it.

Makes about 25 biscuits
100g unsalted butter, very soft
100g caster sugar
1 organic egg
200g Italian 00 flour
½ tsp baking powder
pinch of salt
flavouring of your choice
   (see introduction, above)
edible silver balls, to decorate
   (optional)

Cream the butter and sugar together in a large mixing bowl and, when pale and forming soft peaks, beat in the egg. Then add the flour, baking powder, salt and flavouring and beat until the mixture comes together in a soft dough. Cut the dough in half and roll each half out into a circle of about 3mm thickness.

Line 1 or 2 baking trays with parchment paper. Cut the rolled-out dough into shapes, flouring the cutter as often as is necessary. Knead together the remaining bits of dough and roll again until you have used up all the dough. When all the biscuits are ready on the trays, put them in the fridge and leave for some 30 minutes.

Preheat the oven to 180°C/gas mark 4.

Bake in the oven for 10 minutes, but check after 8. They may even take 12 minutes; it all depends on the shape and thickness of the pastry. The biscuits are ready when they become golden around the edges.

Take the trays out of the oven and let the biscuits cool for about 10 minutes, before transferring to a wire rack, using a spatula. Ask your Coco to sprinkle them with some silver balls or any other decorations she chooses, and then leave them to cool completely. If your Coco hasn't greedily eaten them all, store them in a tin.

Chocolate crispies

These hardly deserve a mention in any cookery book, but Coco insisted I put the recipe in. She said that everybody loves these crispies but often they don't think of making them or they make them with dark chocolate, which is no good. When I said that I don't like them, even with milk chocolate, she rebuked me dismissively, 'Ah, but you are Italian!'

Makes about 30
100g milk chocolate
25g unsalted butter
50g Rice Krispies

Melt the chocolate and the butter together in a heavy-based pan, then spoon in the Rice Krispies and mix thoroughly to coat them all over with the buttery chocolate.

Set out paper cases on a baking tray or plates and spoon a small tablespoon of the mixture into each case. When they are cold, put them in the fridge for an hour or so to set. So quick and easy, these are perfect for children's parties.

Scotch pancakes

I like these thicker pancakes more for a sweet treat, while I prefer the English thin pancakes when I want a savoury dish.

When Coco was very young, she just chose the topping, as she did when we made *pizzelle* (see p.32). Now that she is 12, she makes these from scratch by herself and I choose my own toppings. We pick from: maple syrup, Nutella, crème de marrons, lemon curd and sliced bananas sprinkled with ground cinnamon. My granddaughter Nell's favourite topping is the following one with ricotta.

Makes about 20 pancakes,
    7cm in diameter
200g Italian 00 flour
3 tbsp icing sugar
1½ tsp baking powder
pinch of salt
350ml semi-skimmed milk,
    at room temperature
20g unsalted butter, melted
2 organic eggs, lightly beaten
flavouring of your choice
    (choose from: grated rind
    of ½ organic lemon, a few
    drops vanilla extract or
    pinch of ground cinnamon)

Sieve the flour, icing sugar, baking powder and salt into a large mixing bowl, then pour over them the milk, butter, eggs and your chosen flavouring and gently whisk together until well combined. Leave on one side to rest for at least half an hour.

Heat a large flat griddle or cast-iron frying pan. When hot, pour in 2 tablespoons of the batter for each pancake. (You can cook more than one pancake at a time, depending on the size of your pan, but space them well apart.) Don't worry if the edges look a bit frayed, they will be fine when you turn the pancakes over. Cook until the tops of the pancakes are speckled with bubbles, then turn them over with a spatula and fry the other side until golden. Keep the pancakes hot in a warm oven while you finish cooking the rest.

For the ricotta topping:
Beat 5 or 6 teaspoons maple syrup in a tub of ricotta until well amalgamated. Use a fork, not a spoon, which can break through the ricotta much better. Taste and add more maple syrup if you wish, then spread a spoonful over each pancake. Nell flavours her pancake batter with 2 pinches ground cinnamon, which is an ideal combination with the maple syrup.

Palline di cioccolato

Chocolate balls

I used to make these chocolate balls with my sons when they were very young. At that time, my repetoire of Italian recipes was very much alive as I still remembered vividly all the good things I helped to make as a child. Somehow, over the years, I forgot about these delicious *palline,* until one day a few years ago I came across them while looking through my mother's old recipe books, and I resurrected them. My grandchildren were just the right age to mess about in the chocolate and butter mixture with their little hands, and to shape the balls and lick their fingers.

Makes about 24 little balls
50g peeled almonds
100g unsalted butter, at room
    temperature
100g granulated sugar
yolk of 1 organic egg
50g best unsweetened cocoa
    powder, sifted
1 tbsp dark rum (or 1 tbsp orange
    flower water)
50g digestive biscuits
30–40g desiccated coconut

Preheat the oven to 180°C/gas mark 4.

Spread the almonds on a baking tray and toast them in the oven for about 10 minutes, until they become just golden and you can smell their aroma.

Put the butter and the sugar in the bowl of a food processor and whiz until creamy. Slide the egg yolk into the mixture through the funnel and whiz again. Add the cocoa powder, a tablespoon at a time, while the machine is on. The mixture will become very hard to mix, so add the rum or the orange flower water. I always use rum, because none of my young eaters ever objected to the faint flavour of alcohol. Spoon the mixture into a bowl.

Grind the toasted almonds in the small bowl of the food processor until the bits are the size of grains of rice and then mix them into the butter mixture. Use a fork to do this; it is more efficient because the prongs of the fork can break through the butter mixture far more easily than a spoon.

Next, put the biscuits into the small bowl of the food processor and blast until they too are the size of grains of rice. Mix them into the butter mixture. Spread the coconut onto a plate . . . and now it is time for your Coco to enjoy herself shaping the balls and licking her fingers.

Pick up small pieces of the mixture and roll them in your hands, shaping them into small balls. Moisten your hands occasionally – it makes the rolling easier. It is a very rich mixture so I make each ball quite small, the size of a round walnut, if there is such a thing. When all the balls are shaped, roll them in the coconut and place them neatly on a plate. Cover with clingfilm and chill until you are ready to eat them.

Pineapple daisies

This doesn't quite deserve to be called a recipe – it was just an idea I had once to encourage Johnny, my grandson, to eat some fruit. That was some 10 years ago and since then I have made these daisies with Coco and her sister Kate, too, when they were little. Coco liked making these more than eating them, but I tried to stipulate the condition: she made it, hence she must eat it.

Serves 6
1 large pineapple
1 kiwi fruit
2 tsp lemon juice
3 tsp caster sugar

Cut off the top and bottom of the pineapple and then cut all the skin away. Remove the skin eyes with the point of a sharp knife - not an easy job - and then cut the pineapple into 6 slices. Peel the kiwi and cut this too into 6 slices. Now you must remove the core in the middle of each pineapple slice. I use an apple corer.

Take a round dish and place the pineapple slices all around it. Your little Coco can now put the kiwi slices in the centre of the pineapple slices to make the daisies.

Put the lemon juice into a small bowl and mix in the sugar. Drizzle this mixture over the fruit, and then cover the dish with clingfilm and put it in the fridge for an hour or so. The lemon and sugar will bring out the flavour of the fruit.

Sweet milk gnocchi

This pudding is to a Northern Italian child what rice pudding is to an English child: a sweet, soft, eggy mixture which can be eaten by itself or with some stewed fruit. It used to be one of my favourites, a real treat, since puddings do not appear very often in an Italian home.

Now it is one of Coco's favourite puddings. The first time I made it for her I followed my mother's recipe; it was a very sweet pud and Coco was ecstatic. I cut down the sugar and Coco is still ecstatic, although when she makes it with me, she always asks for 'one more spoonful of sugar, please'.

If I serve the gnocchi by themselves I like to substitute the lemon zest with either the seeds of ½ vanilla pod or with ½ teaspoon ground cinnamon. 'Very yummy surrounded by a chocolate sauce,' suggests Coco (see p.165).

We usually spoon the custard into silicone moulds of different shapes – hearts are great favourites, and the yellow hearts look lovely surrounded by the poached blueberries on p.60. But you can also spread the mixture and let it chill in a single shape and then cut it into squares, rectangles or rounds.

Makes 12 hearts
4 organic eggs
175g caster sugar
50g cornflour, sifted
500ml single cream
zest of 1 organic lemon

Beat the eggs with the sugar until creamy. Put the cornflour into a small bowl, add a little of the cream (about 4 tablespoons) and beat well to form a liquid paste. Now pour the cornflour paste into the egg and sugar mixture and beat well to incorporate. Pour in the rest of the cream, add the lemon zest, and continue beating until the mixture is well blended.

Transfer to a saucepan and cook over a very low heat, stirring the whole time, until the mixture is quite thick and the first bubbles break the surface (about 5 minutes). Cook for a couple more minutes while still stirring.

Moisten your silicone moulds with a drop of cold water and fill each of them with the custard. Give a wet teaspoon to your Coco and ask her to spread the mixture all round each mould, so that every corner is filled. When the shapes are cold, put them in the fridge. They can stay there for a day or two. I like to serve these gnocchi with the softened fruit in the next recipe.

Poached blueberries

Serves 4–6
250g blueberries
2 tbsp caster sugar
juice of 1 lemon

Rinse the berries under cold water, put them in a pan and add the sugar. Cook until the berries break up. Mix in the lemon juice and that's it. Let the berries get cold in the fridge and then serve them in a bowl or let your Coco spoon them around the gnocchi hearts (see p.58). Coco likes to draw patterns with the juice around the hearts 'as they do in the restaurant', she says.

2
Chopping
& Cutting

By the age of 6, Coco had moved on and was able to really help with some of the preparation in the kitchen. I began to trust her enough to let her do more complicated tasks, still all under my watchful eye. She loved to make aubergine parcels or herby rolls, to dip pieces of food in egg yolk and then 'pat pat pat' in the breadcrumbs, and to mix dough and cake batter. And best of all she loved making pasta, which all my grandchildren, and my children before them, would have liked to make far more often than I was ever prepared to do.

Egg pasta

'Johnny, Johnny stop it. Don't go so fast!' screams Coco at her brother who is turning the handle of the pasta machine as quickly as he can. Like most boys, Johnny is fascinated with the machine itself and doesn't care about the result. Coco is furiously trying to disentangle the tagliatelle that roll out of the machine cutter at full speed, too fast for her to wrap them carefully around her hands to make the pretty nests she wants to achieve.

At the other end of the table, Nell and her friend Paloma are working in perfect harmony. Paloma turns the handle of their machine slowly, allowing Nell to make the little nests, which they admire together, tying up the odd strand of pasta and pushing it neatly in place.

This was a scene in my kitchen a few years ago.

Whenever I've made pasta with children they've found it enormous fun. With them, I have always made it with the hand-cranked machine and never attempted to make it by hand because, if it's difficult enough for me, I do not think that any child would be able to roll out the very stiff dough as thin as it needs to be.

My children started to help me very early, but by the age of 6 or 7 any child should be able to enjoy the process of making pasta and, even more, eating the result of their labour. They will soon be able to appreciate how delicious home-made pasta is, so much better than shop-bought fresh pasta.

Makes enough pasta for
    4–5 portions of tagliatelle,
    lasagne or ravioli
300g Italian 00 flour
3 organic eggs
1 tsp sea salt

Put the flour on your work surface, keeping a little mound on the side. Ask your Coco to make a well in the middle of the flour and then to crack the eggs into it and add the salt. Now give your Coco a fork and ask her to break up and lightly beat the eggs while gathering flour from the wall of the well. See that she does it slowly and carefully, because if the wall breaks, a flow of egg will escape and run at full speed along the work surface – great fun but not so easy to capture it and clean afterwards. Done slowly, the mixture will become stiffer and stiffer and you will soon be able to gather it up into a messy ball. Add some of the flour you've set aside if necessary. All of this can be done in the food processor, but it wouldn't be such fun.

Wash your and your helper's hands and scrape

clean all the bits from the work surface. Having done that, knead the dough until it sticks together (just 2–3 minutes) and then you can start using the machine, which not only stretches out the dough but also kneads it. Pull off a piece of dough the size of an orange, while keeping the rest of the dough between 2 plates, and push it through the rollers set at the widest opening. Do that 7 times, each time folding the piece of dough and turning it over. This turning is necessary in order to knead the dough evenly. Then reduce the width of the rollers by one notch and pass the sheet of dough through it without folding it. Repeat this process, reducing the width by one notch each time. For tagliatelle or pappardelle I stop at the last but one setting; for lasagne, *capelletti* ('little hats') and ravioli I roll the sheet to the last setting; while if I want to make *tonnarelli* (square spaghetti), I stop at the fourth setting. Whenever the dough sticks, dust it lightly with flour.

The following are operations which children love doing:

For tagliatelle, or *tonnarelli*, you must let the sheets of dough dry a little or the machine won't be able to cut the dough. Lay each sheet of rolled-out pasta on a clean tea towel, letting about a third of its length hang down over the edge of the work surface. Leave them until the pasta is dry and slightly leathery to the touch. I ask Coco to turn the sheets over halfway through and I always call her at the end to feel whether they are dry. It is impossible to say exactly how long it will take; it depends on the temperature and the humidity of the room and the texture of the pasta. But it usually takes around 20–30 minutes. Coco then puts the sheets through the cutter and, if the strands are dry enough, she makes little nests by wrapping the strands around her hands. If the strands are still slightly damp, we

spread them on the tea towels to dry some more.

The cutting is Coco's favourite operation. She likes to have her sister Kate or a friend turn the handle of the machine, while she catches the long strands coming out of the cutting rollers.

If you want to make pappardelle, start immediately cutting the dough after you have finished rolling it out to its last but one notch. Give your Coco a pastry wheel and ask her to cut each sheet of pasta into strips about 2cm wide. She'll love to do that.

For lasagne, *cappelletti* or ravioli you must not let the pasta sheets dry at all. For lasagne cut the sheets into about 10cm lengths, while for ravioli or *cappelletti* leave the sheets as they are and proceed to make the shapes straightaway, or the pasta will dry out and will not be pliable enough to make and seal them.

This might seem a very laborious performance, but I can assure you that, after the first few trials, you'll be able to make long pasta or lasagne for the family in half an hour – though ravioli would take longer and *cappelletti* even longer, but they are the biggest treat for you to make, of course. The following are Coco's favourite dressings, and her favourite recipes for lasagne, *cappelletti* and ravioli.

Coco's favourite sauces for tagliatelle or pappardelle

Coco loves her tagliatelle or pappardelle dressed with one of these 3 pestos: nettle, basil and wild garlic. I have to agree that they are excellent sauces for home-made pasta. Besides, for Coco and Kate there is the added pleasure of collecting the herbs. During the nettle season, they arm themselves with rubber gloves and a basket and off they go. No lack of nettles in their garden or down the lane. And wild garlic flourishes on the bank of a nearby stream. Both herbs are ready more or less at the same time, in April. We make the pesto in the liquidiser, which Coco and Kate like to control.

Each of these pestos makes enough to dress tagliatelle or pappardelle made with 300g Italian 00 flour and 3 eggs (see p.66), or 400g dried egg tagliatelle.

When you cook home-made tagliatelle remember that they take no more than 2 minutes to be ready. Also, reserve a mugful of the pasta water before draining it. You will need to add an extra 2 or 3 tablespoons of water to the pesto since home-made pasta absorbs sauce very quickly and needs quite a bit of liquid.

Nettle pesto

Come April, the garden is full of nettles. They are not pretty but they are good to eat. I think of nettle risotto and nettle pesto and ask Coco or Kate to collect some. Kate loves anything to do with nature, from picking up big black spiders from my bathroom before I can kill them, to sneaking into bushes to pick gooseberries, to going out with a pair of gloves and picking nettle tops for this ever-popular pesto.

Nettles must be eaten in the spring, when young and tender, and only the tops should be picked; later they lose that peculiar delicate flavour which always reminds me of fig milk. (I don't think you can find them in the shops, so you will have to go outside and hunt for them.) Make the pesto and store it in the fridge, where it can stay for a good month or so. If you don't intend to use it straightaway, do not add the cheese, because it will lose flavour. Mix it in just before you use the pesto.

100g nettle tops
2 tbsp fresh pistachio nuts,
    shelled
1 garlic clove
4 tbsp walnut oil
6 tbsp mild extra-virgin olive oil
30g Parmigiano-Reggiano,
    freshly grated
sea salt and freshly ground
    black pepper, to taste

Wearing a pair of rubber gloves, wash the nettles and blanch them in a cupful of boiling salted water. Cook until tender – about 5 minutes – and drain them.

When they are cool enough, squeeze all the water out – once cooked they don't sting any more. Put the pistachio nuts in a food processor together with the nettles and the garlic. Season with salt and pepper and whiz while adding the 2 oils through the funnel. If you're using the pesto right away, add the cheese now. And don't forget to ask your young chef to taste.

When the tagliatelle are cooked, reserve a mugful of the pasta water and mix it into the pesto. Then add the drained pasta, toss well and add more water if necessary.

Basil pesto

No gathering of wild basil on the hills of Dorset where I live, but every now and then there is enough basil in the vegetable garden for a lovely pesto. When you collect basil, cut off the top and with any luck it will grow again.

60g basil leaves
1 or 2 garlic cloves
30g pine nuts
1 tsp sea salt
120ml mild extra-virgin olive oil
4 tbsp freshly grated
    Parmigiano-Reggiano
4 tbsp freshly grated aged
    pecorino
2 tbsp Greek yoghurt (optional)

Put the basil, garlic, pine nuts and salt in a food processor and whiz at high speed until well blended. Add the oil slowly through the funnel. Spoon the mixture into a bowl and then mix in the cheeses and the yoghurt (if using).

Coco likes to make pesto in the mortar, round and round with the pestle until '*Ecco fatto*' she used to say when the pesto was ready. To do this, put the basil leaves, pine nuts and salt in the mortar and grind against the side with the pestle while adding a little of the olive oil. When the pesto is made, mix in the cheeses and the remaining oil.

When your pasta is cooked, mix 3 or 4 tablespoons of the reserved pasta water into the pesto and then add the drained pasta. Toss well and add more pasta water if necessary to get the right consistency.

Wild garlic pesto

This is a very strong pesto. I put a lump of butter in the serving bowl with it and use 2 heaped tablespoons of pesto for 4 servings of pasta. But that's me and Coco – her brother Johnny always adds some extra pesto to his plate. And you too might like the garlic flavour more than we do. So, this quantity makes more pesto than you actually need to dress enough pasta for 4–5 people.

200g wild garlic leaves
50g flat-leaf parsley
2 slices good-quality white
    bread, crusts removed
2 tsp Dijon mustard
1 tsp sea salt flakes
freshly ground black pepper,
    to taste

Wash the garlic leaves thoroughly (dogs love walking through wild garlic, often lifting their legs in appreciation of the scent), drain and dry them and put them with the parsley in the bowl of a food processor. Whiz for 2 or 3 seconds until broken down. Break the bread into morsels and add to the bowl, together with the mustard, salt and pepper. Whiz until the ingredients are well amalgamated. Call your Coco for the final judgement on the seasoning and don't forget to add some of your reserved pasta water to the final dressing.

Ravioli and cappelletti

Children love to make ravioli and *cappelletti*, which means 'little hats' because they do indeed look like peaked caps. The shape and the name themselves are fascinating to any child.

Coco and I, plus the other members of the family, had a discussion about which ravioli and *cappelletti* we wanted to include in this book. We like ravioli stuffed with many kinds of ingredients. Eventually we narrowed the list down to these two, one for each shape, first because they are indeed good and, second, because the stuffing is relatively simple and quick to make, which compensates for the time spent on the pasta. And here they are, starting with ravioli which are easier to make.

Butternut ravioli

Serves 3–4

For the stuffing:

400g butternut squash,
    seeds removed
400g sweet potatoes
3 tbsp ricotta
3 tbsp chopped flat-leaf parsley
yolk of 1 organic egg
½ tsp grated nutmeg
sea salt, to taste
olive oil, for greasing

For the ravioli:

pasta made with 200g
    Italian 00 flour and 2 eggs
    (see p.66 for method)
2 tbsp salt
1 tbsp oil

First make the stuffing, which I find I always have to do by myself because it is not particularly interesting for a child.

Preheat the oven to 220°C/gas mark 7. Line a baking tray with foil and brush the foil with a little olive oil.

Cut the squash into big pieces and put them on the tray. Pierce the sweet potatoes with a metal skewer and place them on the tray too. Turn the heat down to 180°C/gas mark 4 and bake until the vegetables are soft. The butternut squash will take less than the potatoes, about 40 minutes. Remove it and set aside while the potatoes finish cooking (approximately another 20 minutes). Cut the sweet potatoes in half and scoop out the flesh. Do the same with the butternut squash. Purée both vegetables through a food mill or a potato ricer, into a saucepan. Coco has always enjoyed turning the handle of the food mill, but is not so keen on the potato ricer; halfway through she usually asks me to finish the hard work. Can't blame her. Put the saucepan on the heat and cook for 2 or 3 minutes, while mixing constantly. This heating will dry out the mixture.

Mix in all the other ingredients, except of course the pasta, and then get a teaspoon and ask your Coco to check the salt.

Prepare the pasta as directed on p.66 and proceed to stuff each sheet of dough as it comes out of the rollers, keeping the rest of the dough covered by a bowl or wrapped in clingfilm. Trim one edge of a sheet with a knife or a pastry wheel. Give a teaspoon to your Coco and ask her to place heaped teaspoons of the filling in a straight line about 3cm from the trimmed edge and about 4cm apart. Having done that, fold the strip of pasta over and press down at the edge and between each mound of the filling. Cut between each mound so that each *raviolo* will have 3 cut edges. Press them firmly together, moistening the edges, if necessary, with damp fingers. Roll out another strip of pasta and do the same thing all over again until all the pasta is filled, a job all children love.

To cook the ravioli, bring a large saucepan of water to the boil. Add the 2 tablespoons salt and 1 tablespoon oil and then gently slide in the ravioli. After the water has come back to the boil, cook them for about 3 minutes. Lift them out with a large slotted spoon or drain though a sieve and transfer them to a bowl in which you have already put the dressing (see below). Mix carefully and serve them straight away, nice and hot.

Mine and Coco's favourite dressing for this ravioli is butter, unsalted of course, melted until it has reached that lovely deep hazelnut colour, and Parmesan. You need to use quite a lot – about 75g butter and the same amount of cheese and half a dozen fresh sage leaves snipped in. Another favourite is the same amount of butter, melted but not browned, which I pour over the ravioli and then I sprinkle with 2 tablespoons Parmesan, 1 tablespoon caster sugar and 1 teaspoon ground cinnamon.

Cappelletti with ricotta and herb stuffing

Serves 5-6

For the stuffing:

500g ricotta

100g fresh herbs, finely chopped
(parsley, marjoram, thyme,
sage, rosemary, borage,
chives, rocket, summer
savory and whatever you
have in the garden)

100g Parmigiano-Reggiano,
freshly grated

rind of 1 organic lemon, grated

1 garlic clove, crushed

2 organic eggs

sea salt and freshly ground
black pepper, to taste

For the cappelletti:

pasta made with 300g
Italian 00 flour and 3 eggs
(see p.66 for method)

2 tbsp salt

1 tbsp oil

The stuffing is extremely quick to make. Just put the ricotta in a bowl and mix well. Add all the other ingredients while you or your Coco goes on beating. Taste and check the seasoning.

Now make the pasta and work on one sheet of pasta at a time, keeping the rest of the dough wrapped in clingfilm or covered by a bowl. Cut each sheet of pasta into about 4cm squares and ask your Coco to put ½ teaspoon of the stuffing bang in the middle of each square. Fold each square diagonally in half, forming a triangle. Press down firmly to seal the edges and then, with the thumb and index finger of one hand, pick the triangle up by one of the corners of the long base, with the tip of the triangle pointing upwards. Now the difficult bit. Grasp the other corner of the base with the other hand and wrap the triangle around the index finger of the first hand until the 2 corners of the triangle meet. Press them hard together, and see that the peak stands upright against your index finger. Difficult, I agree, but fun. Set all the *cappelletti* out in a row on a dry tea towel. When you have finished the pasta, start cooking the *cappelletti* or have a well-earned rest with a cup of tea or coffee and then cook them. It does not matter if they get dry.

Cook the *cappelletti* in the same way as the ravioli (p.76), adding the salt and oil to the cooking water. Drain, as before, and dress them with melted butter, cheese and sage to which you can add 1 crushed clove of garlic. Or just use a simple tomato sauce like that on p.34.

Mushroom soup

In my experience soup is not a favourite with children. The consequence is that it is difficult to get them to help you to make it. And yet soups are wonderful; they are nourishing and satisfying, they can prepare the palate for subsequent pleasures, and they can cool you in the summer and warm you in the winter.

To encourage Coco, I began with this mushroom soup for the simple reason that she adores mushrooms of any variety.

This is the dish that we most often make when we come back from a fungi foray with our baskets full of all kinds of specimens. But we have also made it with cultivated mushrooms – the chestnut sort are best – to which we add dried porcini mushrooms for a stronger flavour. If you are making the soup with wild fungi, you don't need the dried porcini.

Serves 4

about 150g wholemeal bread
20g dried porcini mushrooms
100ml full-fat milk
250g cultivated mushrooms
75g unsalted butter
1 shallot, chopped
2 tbsp chopped flat-leaf parsley
generous grating of
    fresh nutmeg
1.2 litres vegetable or
    chicken stock
sea salt and freshly ground
    pepper, to taste
4 tbsp soured cream
    (if your Coco likes it),
    to serve

Preheat the oven to 150°C/gas mark 2. Break the bread into small pieces and put it on a baking tray. Place the tray in the oven and bake for about 15 minutes until the bread has dried up and is beginning to crisp. Put the bread in a food processor and whiz until it forms coarse, not fine crumbs.

Put the porcini in a small saucepan, cover with the milk and bring to the boil. Then turn the heat off and set aside for 15 minutes or so.

Coarsely chop the cultivated mushrooms. (That is Coco's job.) Heat the butter in your soup pot until it begins to sizzle, throw in the shallot and half the parsley and sauté for some 5 minutes. After that add the breadcrumbs and fry them for 3 or 4 minutes, stirring the whole time. Season with the nutmeg and with salt and pepper to taste.

Drain the porcini, reserving the milk, and throw them in the breadcrumb pan. Sauté for a minute or 2 and then add the chopped mushrooms and cook for 3 or 4 minutes. Pour over them the reserved milk and the stock. Mix well, bring to the boil and simmer, uncovered, for a good 30 minutes. Put the soup in a food processor or liquidiser, or mash it with a stick blender – by far the easiest way, if you have one, and also the most fun for your Coco. Mix in the remaining parsley.

Ladle the soup into 4 bowls and spoon 1 tablespoon of the soured cream into the middle of each bowl, if you are using it.

Farfalle with ham and peas

To be honest the following recipe is not a dish I have made *with* Coco, but rather a dish I have made *for* Coco, and all the children in my life, in anticipation of applause and happiness at the table. It's a meal that I knock up at the last minute. One of the grandchildren pops in and I have nothing to give them. But I often have a piece of boiled gammon, a slice or two of ham or a piece of pickled tongue, or some smoked salmon, or prawns in the freezer, and our supper is done – as nutritious as it is delicious.

Pasta is nowadays an essential in most kitchen store cupboards (I always wonder what English children ate before the 80s when pasta became popular in this country), as are frozen peas in the freezer. Don't worry if you don't have farfalle; tagliatelle or penne are good too. However, somehow farfalle is the perfect shape for these rather delicate sauces and they are a popular choice for children.

Serves 4–5

50g unsalted butter
1 shallot, very finely chopped
180g ham or tongue
150g frozen peas
½ tsp vegetable stock powder, such as Marigold Swiss vegetable bouillon
350g farfalle
150ml double cream
sea salt and freshly ground black pepper, to taste
freshly grated Parmigiano-Reggiano, to serve

Heat the butter in a sauté pan and, when its foam begins to subside and it starts to turn a hazelnut colour, throw in the shallot. Sauté gently for 5 minutes or so.

Cut the ham or tongue into short matchsticks and, when the shallot is golden, add to the pan.

Let the mixture fry for a few minutes while you stir it frequently. Spoon in the peas with the ice still around them, sprinkle with the stock powder and season with salt and pepper. Give it a good stir and then put a lid on the pan and cook over a very low heat for 10 minutes. Keep a watch on the sauce and add a little boiling water if it gets too dry. Call your Coco to taste and check the seasoning.

While the sauce is simmering, cook the pasta in the usual way. Drain, and turn it into the sauté pan. Spoon in the cream and stir-fry the whole thing for a minute or so, before you divide it onto the heated plates. Hand around the Parmesan.

My hummus

Years ago I found a recipe called 'Chickpea Salad' in *Diva Cooking* by Victoria Blashford-Snell and Jennifer Joyce, a book full of good and interesting recipes. I made the dish once or twice as it was given in the recipe, but then I began to try to give it my signature. This is certainly not because the original recipe was no good; it is probably better than mine. It is simply because I cannot cook anything by following a recipe step by step. Too boring.

Now when I make this with Coco, we decide what ingredients we want to add; and every time, the hummus has slight variations. Fundamentally, however, it remains the same: a Turkish chickpea purée reimagined by a couple of Italian cooks. Next to the hummus dish I put a plate of pitta bread, which Coco loves to dip into the purée.

Chickpeas have a very high nutritional value. If your children are not keen on meat, give them chickpeas or other pulses, which are just as good a source of protein.

I prefer to make the hummus with dried chickpeas that I soak overnight and then cook. I know it might be an added labour, but the hummus tastes infinitely better when made with dried chickpeas rather than tinned. And, frankly, it is hardly 'labour', since you just soak the chickpeas and go to sleep, then, the next day, you put the chickpeas in a saucepan, cover with water, put the pot on the heat and forget about them for about 2 hours, while you get on with something else. Of course, opening a tin of chickpeas is certainly less demanding and quicker, but it is to the detriment of the dish itself. Yet you might prefer to do that. Just out of pure gastronomic interest, one day make versions of the hummus with the 2 different chickpeas and have a comparative tasting. You will see for yourself what I mean.

Serves 4–5
150g dried chickpeas
   (or 400g tin chickpeas)
1 tbsp bicarbonate of soda
1 tsp sea salt
1 tbsp plain flour
1 onion, unpeeled (but washed)
   and cut in quarters
2 bay leaves
2 garlic cloves

If you are using dried chickpeas, put them in a pot and cover with water. Make a paste with the bicarbonate of soda, salt, flour and a little cold water and spoon it into the pot. This mixture softens the skin of the chickpeas. Mix well and then leave overnight or for about 8 hours. After that, drain and rinse the chickpeas and put them in a pot – earthenware is the best – with the onion, bay leaves and garlic. Cover the pot with a lid and put it on the heat. Bring to the boil and then turn the heat right down. Simmer very gently for about 2 hours until soft. The chickpeas might need even longer to cook properly; they should be quite soft for a good hummus. Drain

For the dressing:
2 red chillies, seeded
1 garlic clove
½ red onion
small bunch of fresh coriander,
    without the stalks
a few sprigs fresh mint,
    with stalks removed
rind and juice of
    ½ organic lemon
4 tbsp extra-virgin olive oil
2 tbsp capers, rinsed
50g plain black olives, stoned
    and cut into pieces
sea salt and freshly ground
    black pepper, to taste

them, reserving a mugful or so of the liquid, and put them in a bowl. Fish out the onion, bay leaves and garlic and discard them. (You can keep the rest of the liquid for a vegetable soup.)

Alternatively, if you want to go out, you can leave the chickpeas in a covered pot in a slow oven for 2–2½ hours. First, bring the water to a simmer on the hob, and then put the pot in a low oven. You only need to make sure that, after 5–10 minutes, the water is still simmering.

If you are using tinned chickpeas, just open the tin, drain and rinse the chickpeas under running water. Easier, I have to admit.

Put the chickpeas in the food processor, blitz to a purée and then spoon into a bowl. Now make the dressing. Finely chop the chillies, garlic, onion and herbs and put into a pudding basin. Mix in the lemon rind and juice, season with salt and pepper and gradually add the oil while you beat with a fork. Add the capers and the olives and mix well. Spoon the dressing over the chickpeas and mix again thoroughly. I prefer to use 2 forks rather than 2 spoons, because the forks break through the thick purée more easily. If necessary, add a little of the reserved chickpea liquid, keeping in mind that the purée gets stiffer when it is cold. Now you can have the tasting session and add an extra pinch of salt, 1 or 2 grindings of pepper or a drop more lemon juice, whatever your Coco thinks is needed.

Stuffed vegetables

I began to stuff vegetables with Coco when she was quite young, mainly for two reasons: the first was that her brother Johnny, two years older, hated vegetables and ate them only when they were in some sort of disguise; the second was that I love stuffed vegetables of any sort or denomination and am always trying to find new ways of stuffing them or of improving my old, favourite ways.

Mushroom caps with Ligurian stuffing

The vegetables you can stuff here are: tomatoes, courgettes, aubergines, mushroom caps and peppers. The time to bake the vegetables varies slightly from 30–45 minutes, longer than one expects, since the oven must not be too hot (180°C/gas mark 4) or the vegetables and the stuffing will shrivel up.

You can adapt this stuffing slightly according to what vegetable you're using. For instance, we add mint when it's courgette, a little chilli for peppers, anchovy fillets for aubergines and peppers too, and 1 tablespoon capers for tomatoes. At this stage I used to let Coco choose some of the ingredients to make it more interesting for her, although I always tried to guide her taste. As with anything else they are learning, children like to be gently guided and not be left totally free.

This is Coco's second favourite way to eat mushroom caps, the first being a *cotoletta* – that is, dipped in egg, and then breadcrumbed and fried. The recipe is particularly good if you use porcini or other boletus large caps, but cultivated mushrooms are not bad at all, especially if you add a little dried porcini to the stuffing.

Serves 4

20g dried porcini mushrooms
  (optional)
500g large mushroom caps
1 or 2 garlic cloves
handful of fresh marjoram
45g dried white breadcrumbs
  (see p.12)
pinch of grated nutmeg
5 tbsp extra-virgin olive oil
2 tbsp chopped flat-leaf parsley
sea salt and freshly ground
  black pepper, to taste

If using, soak the dried porcini in a cupful of very hot water for 20–30 minutes. Rinse and dry with kitchen paper. Preheat the oven to 180°C/gas mark 4. Gently wipe the mushroom caps with a damp piece of kitchen paper and detach the stalks. Chop together the dried porcini, mushroom stalks, garlic and marjoram. Transfer to a bowl and mix in the breadcrumbs, nutmeg, and salt and pepper to taste.

Heat 2 tablespoons of the oil in a frying pan and add the breadcrumb mixture. Sauté for 5–7 minutes, stirring frequently. Now it is time for the important tasting session – ask your Coco to check that the seasoning is just right before you go on. Lay the mushroom caps on an oiled baking tray, hollow side up. Sprinkle lightly with salt and then fill them with the crumb mixture. Sprinkle a pinch or two of the chopped parsley on each cap and drizzle with the remaining olive oil. Bake for 30 minutes or so, until the caps are soft. Serve at room temperature.

Aubergine parcels of couscous and prawn

Coco has loved fish, especially seafood, since she was a baby, or let's say a toddler. This delighted me because I share her love and have been able to cook many of my favourite dishes for her. And this is one. Unfortunately, she has recently developed an allergy to aubergine, so, these parcels are out for her, or partly out for her: she scrapes some of the stuffing out of the aubergine slice and gobbles it up with a spoon. Or, if I have time, we make 3 or 4 courgette cups for her, as described at the end of this recipe.

Serves 6

3 aubergines, about 300g each
5 tbsp extra-virgin olive oil
200ml red wine vinegar
2 garlic cloves
sprig of fresh thyme
1 celery stick, sliced
1 fresh red chilli, seeded
  and sliced
3 spring onions, sliced
4 anchovy fillets, chopped
350g raw peeled prawns
350ml boiling water
300g couscous
2 tbsp capers, roughly chopped
  if large
3 tbsp chopped flat-leaf parsley
2 tbsp lemon juice
sea salt and freshly ground
  black pepper, to taste

Wash and dry the aubergines and, with a sharp knife, cut off the ends. Slice the aubergines lengthways into 3mm pieces, more or less the same thickness as a £1 coin. This is a job that no child can do. It is difficult enough for me, and for a child it would be dangerous. You should get between 6 and 10 slices, depending on how fat each aubergine is and also on your dexterity.

With a pastry brush, moisten each side of the slices with some of the olive oil. Now you can either grill the slices on both sides or dry-fry in a hot pan. I prefer to pan-fry them, so that I can catch each slice when it is just ready, soft, but not burnt (about 3 minutes). When all the slices are done, lay them in a dish.

Now make the marinating liquid. Boil the vinegar with 1 garlic clove and the sprig of thyme for 5 minutes and then pour it over the aubergine and leave for 1 hour to absorb the flavour. Turn the slices over halfway through the marinating.

Heat 2 tablespoons of the oil in a sauté pan. Chop or crush the remaining garlic clove and fry together with the celery, chilli, spring onion and anchovy fillets for 5 minutes, turning them over frequently. Add the prawns and the boiling water. Turn the heat down and simmer for 2 minutes, until the prawns change colour.

Put the couscous in a bowl and then strain the prawns over it so that the liquid falls over the couscous

to cover it. Cut the prawns into small bits and set aside together with the vegetable mixture.

When the couscous is cold, break it all up with a fork. Dress it with the remaining oil, the capers and the parsley. Add the prawn bits and the vegetable mixture and mix thoroughly but lightly with 2 forks to break up any lumps. Here is when I ask Coco to taste, add the lemon juice and check the salt and pepper.

Now comes the final preparation, which is the bit the children like best. Lay the aubergine slices on a board and pat them dry with kitchen paper. Place about 1 tablespoon of the couscous mixture over each slice and then roll the slice up Swiss roll fashion. Secure the end with a wooden cocktail stick – and that's it. Serve the rolls on a dish or on individual plates and enjoy them.

Courgette cups

Because of Coco's new allergy to aubergine, we also make these parcels with courgettes – although I think they combine less well with the flavour of the fishy filling. Cut about 6 medium-sized courgettes into 5cm chunks. Steam or boil the chunks and, when just soft enough, scoop out the seedy middle with an apple corer or the pointed handle of a teaspoon, being careful not to go through the bottom of the chunk. Dry each chunk very well inside and out, then pour a little of the marinating vinegar into each courgette cup and leave for 1 hour. After that, empty the cups, dry them out and fill each cup with some of the couscous and prawn stuffing.

Tomatoes stuffed with pasta

These stuffed tomatoes are rather more difficult to make than the tomatoes stuffed with parsley and breadcrumbs on p.85, because they must be carefully prepared so that they can hold the pasta. Coco graduated quite quickly from the first simple dish to this more complicated one. Sometimes she adds pieces of buffalo mozzarella, a few capers or 1 or 2 chopped anchovy fillets to the pasta.

Serves 4

6 large ripe tomatoes
150g small shell pasta
5 tbsp extra-virgin olive oil
2 tbsp chopped flat-leaf parsley
1 tbsp chopped fresh oregano
    or marjoram
1 garlic clove, chopped
pinch or 2 of dried crushed chilli
sea salt and freshly ground
    black pepper, to taste

Wash and dry the tomatoes and then cut off the top of each tomato, which you will use later as a lid. With the handle of a pointed teaspoon scoop out all the seeds and pulp, to make a cup. Sprinkle the inside of each tomato with some salt and put them upside down on a board to drain for half an hour or so. Preheat the oven to 180°C/gas mark 4.

While the tomatoes are draining, cook the pasta in plenty of boiling salted water. Drain into a bowl when it is very al dente since it will cook again inside the tomatoes.

Dress the pasta immediately with 3 tablespoons of the oil and black pepper to taste, and mix in the herbs, garlic, chilli and whatever other bits you have chosen to add. Check the seasoning.

Wipe the inside of each tomato with kitchen paper, then spoon the pasta into each tomato cup and cover with its tomato lid.

Brush a baking tray with some of the remaining oil and place the tomatoes on the tray. Drizzle with what oil you have left and bake for about half an hour. Coco likes them cold; I prefer them hot. Try them both ways and then ask your Coco which she prefers.

Latkes

I learnt to make these potato cakes from my children who, in turn, learnt to make them from their English grandmother. It was one of the very good dishes that Granny produced and my children loved it, as do my grandchildren with whom I have been making them for quite a few years.

To the original Jewish recipe, I have always added my Italian touch, a sprinkling of Parmesan. These latkes might not be traditional any longer, but I prefer them this way.

Makes about 8 latkes
500g old potatoes
1 shallot
½ tsp salt
1 egg
2 tbsp freshly grated
    Parmigiano-Reggiano
2 tbsp dried breadcrumbs
    (see p.12)
2 tbsp chopped flat-leaf parsley
freshly ground black pepper,
    to taste
oil, for frying

Peel the potatoes and grate them in a food processor fitted with the grater disc. Scoop them all out into a bowl and cover them with cold water. This will remove some of the unwanted starch. Finely chop the shallot and any bits of potato that might have come out in slices from the food processor.

Drain the potato mush through a fine sieve. Scoop out handfuls and squeeze the mush hard between your hands to get rid of the liquid and then put it in a bowl. This was one of Coco's favourite tasks – very satisfying work. When the potato has been drained, add all the other ingredients except the oil. Taste and check the seasoning, adding a little pepper if you want. Coco always does. Mix thoroughly with your hands, the best and most-loved tools.

Put enough oil into a heavy-based frying pan to come 1cm up the sides of the pan. When the oil is hot, scoop out some potato mixture with your hands to form little cakes about 8cm round. Slide them gently into the hot oil and fry them, on both sides, about 5 minutes per side. Lift them out with a fish slice and place them on a dish lined with kitchen paper.

Eat the latkes as soon as you can. Like all fritters, they are best straight out of the pan. Coco and I often eat them by themselves, but they are good, too, with the tomato sauce on p.34.

Arancini *Fried rice balls*

I don't think Coco or her siblings started making risotto at the age of 6, but I remember her enjoying watching the making of the *soffritto* – the lightly fried onion base. She was fascinated to see how the sizzling of the butter and oil subsided when we threw in the chopped onion. She loved the slight change in the colour of the onion, then the adding of the rice and, finally, the sizzling noise when I poured in the wine. After the first ladleful of stock went in, the fun was over and she disappeared until the end when I called her to add the butter in little bits and sprinkle the Parmesan. But the pleasure of preparing a risotto came the next day when we made *arancini* with the leftovers.

Arancini can be made with boiled rice as well, which is a far quicker expedient than risotto. And what follows is how I make them when I haven't any leftover risotto. As for the stuffing, when Coco first started helping me she liked to push a pea into each *arancino*, then later she would choose a piece of mozzarella, or a bit of sausage (cooked) or salami. So we changed through the years. And with the passing of time, Coco was able to make the balls, stuff them, coat them and get them totally ready for chilling before we fried them together.

If you don't have any home-made vegetable stock to hand, put 2 or 3 teaspoons of vegetable stock powder in the water (I use Marigold Swiss vegetable bouillon powder).

Makes about 24 *arancini*
300g risotto rice
vegetable stock
4 organic eggs
25g unsalted butter
25g pecorino, freshly grated
25g Parmigiano-Reggiano,
    freshly grated
handful of cooked peas
about 3 tbsp plain flour
about 100g dried unflavoured
    breadcrumbs (see p.12)
100ml olive oil
sea salt and freshly ground
    black pepper, to taste

If you don't have any leftover, cooked risotto, cook the rice in plenty of boiling vegetable stock for about 12 minutes. Drain, reserving the stock for a soup or whatever you like. Tip the rice into a bowl and let it cool a little before adding 2 of the eggs, the butter and the 2 cheeses. Mix very well. We always add a little pepper as well and then taste it to decide if it needs some salt. Let the rice get very cold.

With damp hands pick up handfuls of rice and shape them into balls, each the size of a golf ball. Stick a pea into the middle of each ball. Spread some flour on a plate and quickly roll each ball into it. Break the 2 remaining eggs into a dish and lightly beat them with a fork. Roll each ball in the egg, and then let the excess egg drop back into the dish. Put the breadcrumbs on a plate and coat the balls with them, gently patting them in with your hands. After that line up all the balls on a board and place the board in the fridge for at least 1 hour.

Heat the oil in a large frying pan and when it is quite hot, gently drop in the rice balls. Fry them for about 5 minutes, turning them over so that they cook evenly all over.

We like them hot or cold or halfway in between. Whatever way, they are always good.

Herby rolls

I make these rolls in the spring, when Coco and I can collect all the fresh, young herbs while they are still tender and have a sweet yet distinctive flavour. Which herbs you use, depends on what you can lay your hands on. Some herbs are essential: parsley, sage, rosemary, marjoram and chives; the rest are . . . the more the merrier. I use young nettle tops, young lovage (just a little), fennel, and then I make up the weight with spinach leaves.

Makes 8 rolls

4 tbsp olive oil, plus more
    for greasing
25g green streaky bacon,
    chopped
30g fresh breadcrumbs
    (see p.13)
75g chopped mixed herbs
1 garlic clove, finely chopped
100g ricotta
3 tbsp freshly grated
    Parmigiano-Reggiano
200–250g puff pastry, defrosted
    if frozen
sea salt and freshly ground
    black pepper, to taste

For the glaze:
yolk of 1 organic egg
1 tbsp milk

Heat a frying pan greased with a little oil and, when hot, throw in the bacon. Fry until crisp and then lift it out and set aside. Cut off and throw away the bacon fat. Heat 3 tablespoons of the oil in the same frying pan. Add the breadcrumbs and fry until golden and crisp and then add the herbs and the garlic and sauté for 4 or 5 minutes. Spoon the mixture into a bowl and mix in the ricotta, bacon and the Parmigiano-Reggiano. Mix well with a fork or with your helper's small hands. Season to taste.

Unroll the pastry and spread it out on a floured board. With a lightly-floured rolling pin, thin it out a little and then brush it with the remaining olive oil. Roughly divide the herby bacon mixture into 8 portions. Roll each portion between the palms of your hands into a sausage shape and place them, well spaced out, on the pastry sheet. Cut the pastry surrounding each portion into pieces large enough to wrap around them. Stretch the pastry to cover all the mixture; if the pastry breaks, don't worry, just patch it up; once it's cooked it will not show. Place the rolls on a baking tray.

Your Coco can now lightly mix the egg yolk and the milk together with a fork and then, with a pastry brush, 'paint' the rolls all over with this mixture.

Put the tray in the fridge and leave it while you preheat the oven to 220°C/gas mark 7. When the oven is ready, place the tray in it and bake the rolls for 15–20 minutes until they are golden all over.

Nonna's golden fingers

I don't like shop-bought fish fingers, but Coco loves them, as most children do. So I developed my own that she enjoys making and we both enjoy eating. She even admitted that my fish fingers are better than Bird's Eye's or an equivalent brand. That is why she named them Golden Fingers.

Buy a thick fillet of cod or pollock, or whatever white fish is freshest on the market.

Serves 4

500g fish fillets
1 organic egg
75–100g dried white
   breadcrumbs (see p.12)
3 tbsp olive oil
50g unsalted butter, cut into
   small pieces
sea salt and freshly ground
   black pepper, to taste

Cut the fillets across into even-sized pieces. I make mine about 3cm thick so that they look like the Bird's Eye fingers. Lightly beat the egg with a little salt and pepper. Spread out the breadcrumbs on a board or plate. Now you are ready to start rolling! Dip each fish piece in the egg, hold it up and let all the excess egg drip back into the bowl and then put the fish on the crumbs. Coat it on every side, patting the crumbs down into the fish – a job for little hands. If you have time, put the coated pieces in the fridge for at least half an hour; they harden up, which makes it easier to fry them.

Put a frying pan on the heat, one large enough for the fish fingers to sit in a single layer. Pour the oil into the pan and tilt it so that the fat covers the whole surface evenly. Now lay the fish fingers in the pan and add the pieces of butter here and there. Cook until the undersides of the fingers have formed a golden crust. Then turn them over and fry the other side – it is difficult to state how long you should cook the fish for; it depends on the heat and also on the thickness of the fish. Usually 5–6 minutes is just about right to achieve a lovely golden crust on the outside with perfectly cooked fish inside. When the fish fingers are on her plate, Coco adds tomato ketchup, and never mind my disapproval. But when there is none in the house, which happens quite often, I convince her to put a spoonful of my own tomato sauce (p.34) on the side, or to squeeze some lemon juice over the fish fingers – and she eats it quite happily.

Chicken with breadcrumbs

We had this dish when we were staying with relatives on Lake Como. Coco was not helping in the kitchen then; she was swimming or water-skiing with her friends. But when we all sat down to eat she exclaimed 'Oh, *è squisito*!' – 'Wow, it is delicious. Can I have the recipe please?' Not only is it *squisito*, it is also extremely easy to make.

Serves 6

6 chicken thighs

6 tbsp extra-virgin olive oil

4 tbsp lemon juice

2 garlic cloves, crushed

100g Parmigiano-Reggiano,
    freshly grated

100g dried white breadcrumbs
    (see p.12)

sea salt and freshly ground
    black pepper, to taste

Separate the drumsticks from the upper thighs and put the pieces in a dish. Mix together 2 tablespoons of the oil and 1 tablespoon of the lemon juice. Add the garlic, some pepper and very little salt (the cheese is salty) and then pour this mixture over the chicken. Leave to marinate for an hour or so.

Preheat the oven to 200°C/gas mark 6.

Mix together the cheese and the breadcrumbs and spread them out on a board. Now coat the chicken pieces with this crumb mixture. Get your Coco to pat the mixture firmly all over the pieces. Pour the remaining oil in an oven tray and lay the chicken pieces in it, in a single layer. Turn them over so that they get coated with the oil and then bake for 1 hour. Halfway through the cooking, spoon the remaining lemon juice all over the chicken. You don't need to turn the pieces over during the cooking, just move them gently if they get stuck to the tray.

Rabbit with onions

My children and grandchildren never minded eating 'bunnies'. Frankly, I cannot see why some people can eat a leg of lamb or a roasted chicken without any qualms and then make a fuss at the thought of eating rabbits. If one is a vegetarian, that's all well and good, but an animal is an animal. But let's get back to cooking and stop preaching.

In the proper Italian tradition, I have cooked rabbit all my life and enjoy eating it. And so do my family. Having said that, this is not the sort of dish Coco is very keen to cook with me; it's a bit boring for her. Her only contribution is that she suggested we use balsamic vinegar (her favourite) as well as wine vinegar and I think it is an improvement to my original recipe.

I prefer to cook – and also to eat – farmed rabbits. The wild ones can be tricky because you cannot know beforehand how old and tough they are. You can be lucky but you can also find yourself with a piece of old boot full of gun shot to deal with. Buy the back legs; the front ones have hardly any meat on them. And if you object to eating 'bunnies' make the dish with chicken legs.

Serves 4

750g red onions, thinly sliced
25g unsalted butter
60ml olive oil
1 tsp sea salt
100ml beef stock (see p.20)
4 free-range farmed rabbit
    back legs
2 tbsp caster sugar
4 tbsp red wine vinegar
4 tbsp balsamic vinegar
juice of ½ lemon
freshly ground black pepper,
    to taste

Put the onion in a casserole with the butter, oil, teaspoon of salt and half the stock and bring to the boil. Cover the casserole with a lid and cook very slowly for 1 hour, until the onion is reduced to a mush. The heat must be very low (I use a heat diffuser plate) and, if necessary, add a little more stock during the cooking.

Preheat the oven to 150°C/gas mark 2.

Wash and dry the rabbit legs and add to the casserole. Turn the heat up a little and cook for 5 minutes, turning the legs over a couple of times. Sprinkle with the sugar and pour in the 2 vinegars and the lemon juice and season with plenty of pepper. Bring back to the simmer, turn the rabbit pieces over, then place the covered casserole in the oven and cook until the rabbit is done – about 45 minutes to 1 hour. The meat should not offer any resistance when you pierce it with a fork.

The best accompaniment to this rabbit is buttery, mashed potatoes – one of most children's favourite vegetables.

Florentine eggs

In the late summer and autumn months my daughter's vegetable garden is invaded by spinach. I cannot bear to see it going to waste so my diet consists of anything with spinach in it or just spinach steamed and generously dressed with my best extra-virgin olive oil and lemon juice.

This is a quick alternative to the usual pasta when one of the grandchildren drops in for supper. I send her out to pick the spinach and I can produce this healthy dish in the same time it takes to make a bowl of pasta. For serving, I fry 4 slices of bread and place the spinachy eggs on top of them. A complete and nourishing meal.

Serves 4

1kg spinach
2 tbsp olive oil
50g unsalted butter
1 garlic clove, crushed
pinch or 2 of grated nutmeg
50g Parmigiano-Reggiano,
    freshly grated
4 organic eggs
sea salt and freshly ground
    black pepper, to taste

Preheat the oven to 200°C/gas mark 6.

Pick over the spinach leaves and discard the tougher stems. Wash them in plenty of cold water and put them straight into a large cooking pot without draining – the water that clings to them is quite enough to cook them in. Put the pot on a high heat and cook, uncovered, until the spinach is tender, about 2 or 3 minutes, turning it over 3 or 4 times. Drain and, wearing a pair of rubber gloves, squeeze out all the water.

Now I call Coco for the part she likes. Cut the spinach roughly into strips. Put the oil and half the butter with the garlic into a frying pan and, when hot, add the spinach and fry for 4–5 minutes, turning it over often.

Take the pan off the heat and mix in the nutmeg, cheese and salt and pepper. Now it is time to taste. Butter a shallow oven dish and spoon the spinach into it, spreading it to cover the whole dish. Make 4 hollows in the spinach with the back of a large metal spoon and break the eggs into these green nests. Put a knob of the remaining butter over each yolk and then place the dish in the hot oven. Bake for 8–9 minutes, until the whites are set but the yolks are still runny.

Meringues

I have never met a child who does not like meringues. (Nor have I met a British child who does not like tomato ketchup. Pity they cannot be combined.) I made meringues with my children throughout their childhood and now I make them with my grandchildren. It is enough for me to say 'I have a few egg whites in the fridge' for one of them to scream 'Meringues!' Coco, being the third child of the family, was able to make them with very well-defined shapes by the age of 6 or thereabouts.

After much trial and error I have settled for Delia's recipe, which, like so many of her recipes, is totally foolproof. 'The secret,' she writes, 'is allowing the meringue to remain in the closed oven after the heat is turned off, so that it partly bakes and then slowly dries out.'

Remember to bring the egg whites to room temperature if they have been kept in the fridge. If cold, they don't whip easily or become as stiff as they should to make good, airy meringues. But also remember to use egg whites that are fresh and not those which have languished at the back of the fridge for weeks. They will not do.

Makes about 12 meringues
whites of 2 organic eggs, at room temperature
120g caster sugar

Preheat the oven to 150°C/gas mark 2.

Place the egg whites in a large bowl and whisk, using an electric whisk, for about 2 minutes, until the whites form stiff peaks. (If you whisk by hand, it will take a lot longer.) Add the sugar, sprinkling it in 1 tablespoon at a time, while you continue whisking. The stiff egg mixture will become softer and glossy.

Line 2 baking trays with parchment paper. Coco sometimes likes to pipe the egg white mixture onto the trays, but usually she prefers to use a dessertspoon which she fills with the sugary mixture and then slides it out with her index finger. (The preference is no doubt due to the fact that her finger finishes in her mouth after each plopping.) I recommend you follow her lead. Leave some space between the blobs.

Place the trays in the oven and immediately turn the oven down to 140°C/gas mark 1 and bake for 40–45 minutes, until the meringues are resistant to the touch. Then turn the heat off and leave the meringues to cool in the oven, which will take about 4 hours, but it does not matter if you leave them longer.

You can store them in a tin, although I find this unnecessary because in my house they will be eaten in one sitting.

What to fill the meringues with is a personal choice – I find whipped cream still the best filling, but Coco also likes to fill them with *dulce de leche* (caramel milk sauce) mixed with some whipped cream, or with Nutella.

Little Mont Blancs

At Christmas we make little Mont Blancs. For these, give a spoon to your Coco and ask her to make a hollow with the back of a dessertspoon in the unbaked meringues. Then bake them as usual and, when cold, fill with this:

Enough to fill 12 meringues
4-5 marrons glacés
50g dark chocolate
 (min. 70% cocoa solids)
250g tin chestnut purée
2 tbsp icing sugar, sifted
2 tbsp fresh pistachio nuts,
 shelled
300ml whipping cream

Break the marrons glacés into small pieces. To melt the chocolate in a microwave oven, break it up into small pieces, put these in a bowl and heat according to your oven's instructions. To melt the chocolate in a bain-marie, put the pieces of chocolate into a heatproof bowl and sit this over a pan of simmering water for about 10–15 minutes. Don't let the bowl touch the water. Spoon the melted chocolate into a bowl and mix in the chestnut purée and about half the sugar. Now it is time for your Coco to taste; she might like a little more chocolate.

Put the pistachio nuts into boiling water for about 30 seconds and then drain, peel and dry them with kitchen paper. Whip the cream to form soft peaks and fold in the remaining icing sugar. Now the filling is ready to be piled on the meringues in this order: first the 'earth' (the chocolate/chestnut purée), then the rocks (the pieces of marrons glacés) with some bushes here and there (the pistachios), and on top the 'snow' (the cream). Great fun.

Pineapple cake

At some point, Kate decided that she didn't like pineapple any more. I love pineapple and find it a very useful fruit: you can always find one in the shops when other fruit is not too plentiful. So I looked through my cookery books to find a recipe that would hide the fruit. And I found this in Lorenza de Medici's *Passion for Fruit*. It was a great success. Coco loves to mix the fruit 'gently gently' into the cake mixture. The cake is best eaten as soon as it is made.

Serves 8

1 pineapple, about 1.5kg
120g Italian 00 flour
2 tsp baking powder
pinch of salt
2 organic eggs
120g golden caster sugar
120g unsalted butter, melted
butter and dried breadcrumbs
   (see p.12), for the tin
icing sugar, for dusting
pouring cream, to serve
   (optional)

Preheat the oven to 180°C/gas mark 4.

Slice off the top and bottom, and then peel the pineapple with a sharp knife and remove all the eyes, which is a very boring job that Coco can at last do well now that she is 12. Cut it into thick slices. Then cut each slice into cubes of about 1cm, discarding the core. Butter a 20cm springform cake tin and sprinkle some dried breadcrumbs into it. Shake it around to cover the buttered surface and then shake off any excess crumbs.

Put the flour, baking powder and salt in a large bowl and mix. Add the eggs and mix well. Add the sugar and, finally, pour in the melted butter and mix very well. When it looks well blended, add the pineapple and mix gently so as not to break the cubes.

Spoon the mixture into the prepared tin and place it in the oven. Bake for 45 minutes, take it out and leave to cool slightly in the tin until warm, then unclip the tin and turn the cake out onto a round dish. Dust the cake with icing sugar before you serve it straight away or at room temperature. You can pass around a jug of pouring cream if your Coco likes it; mine doesn't.

Canary pudding

alias *Il Monte Bianco Dorato*

Some 50 years ago, my sons christened this canary pudding 'The Golden Mont Blanc' because of its shape and colour. I never made many puddings during my first years in England – I still don't, to be honest. Puddings are not in the tradition of everyday cooking in an Italian family. So I learned a few basic ones from my English mother-in-law. I think this one is the 'Canary Pudding' that first appeared in Mrs Beeton's *Everyday Cookery,* together with its companion 'Castle Pudding', but my mother-in-law might well have revisited the original recipe. This, I know, is her recipe, apart from the golden caster sugar, which is relatively new on the market.

Serves 6

120g unsalted butter, at room
    temperature
120g golden caster sugar
2 organic eggs
120g self-raising flour
grated rind of 1 organic lemon
    (reserve juice for the sauce)
1–1½ tbsp full-fat milk
2–3 tbsp golden syrup

For the sauce:
3 tbsp golden syrup
juice of 1 lemon
    (from above lemon)

Cream together the butter and the sugar. Lightly beat the eggs and then add them to the butter mixture alternating with spoonfuls of flour: one of this, one of that. (You can do this in the food processor by putting all the ingredients in together, as Coco does now, because, she says, the butter mixture sometimes splatters everywhere. That happens when the butter is not soft enough.)

Now add the lemon rind and enough milk to make a sloppy consistency and mix well (or, if you are using a food processor, blitz again for a second or two). Generously butter a plastic pudding basin that has an 800ml capacity and a lid. Spoon the 2–3 tablespoons golden syrup into it and then add the sponge mixture. Bang the basin carefully on the work surface to eliminate any air bubbles, put its lid on and place the basin in a large pan. Pour around it enough boiling water to come halfway up the sides of the basin and then cover the saucepan with its lid and steam for 2 hours.

Lift the pudding basin out of the water and take the lid off. Slide a palette knife all around the sides of the pudding and then place a round dish over it and turn the basin over. The pudding should fall out on to the dish straightaway.

Your Coco can make the sauce by gradually adding the lemon juice to the 3 tablespoons golden syrup, stopping when she thinks the sauce is tart enough. Serve straight away, lovely and hot, like a proper old-fashioned steamed pudding.

Soft chocolate nougat

alias *Parrot pudding*

'But, Nonna, you must put parrot pudding in. It is the first pud I learnt to make and the one we all like best,' said Coco when she looked at the final list of recipes for this book. Parrot pudding is the name by which soft nougat is known in our family. This odd name was chosen by my sons, who really loved only 2 puds: canary pudding and this one, which they decided to call 'parrot', because those were the 2 birds they liked best. It certainly is a surprising name for a dark brown pudding that, if anything, looks more like a raven than a parrot. But the name stuck.

Some 50 years later we still make parrot pudding for Christmas for all those who are not keen on Christmas pudding and those who eat both, like me. So I had to include the recipe even though it has appeared in 2 or 3 of my previous books.

I add Cointreau or rum, but if you object to giving children alcohol that has not been cooked, use orange flower water instead.

Serves 8

125g almonds, blanched
200g unsalted butter, softened
200g granulated sugar
100g best-quality unsweetened
   cocoa powder
1 large organic egg
yolk of 1 large organic egg
100g digestive biscuits
3 tbsp Cointreau (or orange
   flower water)
candied flowers and blanched or
   sugared almonds, to decorate

Preheat the oven to 180°C/gas mark 4.

Spread the almonds on a baking tray and bake for 7–10 minutes until they turn golden. Grind them coarsely in a food processor, being very careful to stop blitzing when they resemble grains of rice.

Next, cream together the butter and sugar until light and fluffy. Sieve the cocoa directly over a bowl, a job which will keep your Coco happily occupied for a few minutes. Add the cocoa to the butter and sugar a spoonful at a time and beat hard until it has been completely incorporated. This takes a little time and some beating, but it can be done in a food processor. Lightly beat together the whole egg and the egg yolk and add to the mixture, stirring until well blended.

Crush the biscuits with a rolling pin and add to the mixture together with the ground almonds and the Cointreau (or orange flower water). Mix thoroughly.

Line a 20 x 10cm loaf tin with clingfilm and spoon the mixture into it, pressing down all the time to eliminate any air bubbles and, when it is all in, bang the tin hard on the work surface to settle the mixture. Cover with clingfilm and chill for at least 4 hours.

Get an oval dish and turn the loaf tin upside down over it; lift off the tin and peel away the clingfilm. Your Coco can now decorate the pudding with candied flowers and almonds. She could top it with a rosette of whipped cream as well but, frankly, I find it rich enough without the cream.

Blackberry jelly

'Come on, let's go and pick some blackberries so that we can make blackberry jelly.' With the incentive of this juicy reward, I always manage to get Coco & co. to come with me, armed with plastic bowls and smiles on their faces. We have competitions to see who can fill their bowl the quickest, but then the actual making of the jelly is usually left to me and I can't blame them. Straining berries is rather lengthy and boring.

The recipe here uses the juice that you get after cooking the berries. Of course, the quantity must be adjusted according to how many blackberries you have managed to pick. But I always find that, more or less, this is the result of a good half an hour's picking by 3 people, which is about the right length of time for most children.

For 250–300ml of juice
you will need:
20g gelatine leaves
120–150g caster sugar
juice of 1 lemon

For the blackberry juice:
First rinse the berries under running water. Put them in a pan and cook them over a gentle heat for 2 or 3 minutes. Then strain the berries through a sieve lined with muslin. Let them drip slowly while you press down gently to release more juice

To make the jelly:
Put the gelatine leaves in a dish and cover them with cold water. Leave them for some 20 minutes until they are completely soft and pliable.

Put the sugar and 100ml water in a saucepan and bring slowly to the boil. Simmer until the sugar has completely dissolved, stirring the whole time. Now squeeze all the water out of the gelatine leaves and add the leaves to the sugar syrup. Stir constantly while the gelatine dissolves, then remove from the heat and mix in the strained blackberry juice and lemon juice. Stir well and taste, remembering that food served cold needs stronger flavouring, in this case the sugar. Spoon the mixture into the prettiest bowls you have and chill for at least 6 hours.

Some children love to swirl whipped cream over the top.

Almond kisses

Maybe it was their Italian name, *baci di dama* or Lady's kisses, but these biscuits from Piedmont have always been a favourite of my sons. We made them often and developed new 'kisses', as you'll see in the recipes that follow.

Now, as with all my Italian dishes, I make *baci di dama* with Coco and Kate, although they don't seem to share the same enthusiasm for the biscuits as their uncles did. I don't know why. But I love them.

If I have time, I make these *baci di dama* with my unpeeled almonds from Sicily, not only because they are better quality but also because my grandchildren love to slip the skin off the nuts. If you are short of time, you can use ground almonds; but the fun of 'undressing' the almonds would be lost.

Makes about 35 biscuits

120g unpeeled almonds
120g caster sugar
120g unsalted butter, at room
    temperature and cut into
    small pieces
1 tsp pure vanilla extract
pinch of salt
120g Italian 00 flour, sifted
100g best-quality dark chocolate
    (min. 70% cocoa solids)
butter, for greasing

Preheat the oven to 180°C/gas mark 4.

Put the almonds into a pan of boiling water and leave them for 30 seconds. With a slotted spoon lift out a few at a time and spread them on a sheet of kitchen paper. As soon as you can touch them, take each almond in turn between your thumb and index finger and squeeze – the hotter they are the easier it is to 'undress' them. The nut will shoot out leaving the skin in your hand.

Spread the peeled almonds on a baking tray and place the tray in the oven. Leave for about 8 minutes until the nuts become golden at the edges and they release that wonderful aroma.

Put the almonds in a food processor, add 2 tablespoons of the sugar and blitz to a grainy powder. The sugar absorbs the oil released by the almonds and helps prevent them from becoming too powdery. Add the rest of the sugar, the butter, vanilla and salt and blitz again until creamy. With the machine running, spoon the flour into the bowl through the funnel. When a soft dough forms, scoop it into a bowl and give it a final thorough and energetic stir.

Now you can have your Coco's help. Pick up small

pieces of dough, each the size of a cherry, and roll them into balls between the palms of your floured hands. Place them on a buttered baking tray – or trays – spacing them about 2cm apart to leave them room to expand. Bake for 12–15 minutes, until golden, and then let them cool a little on the tray. Only when they are cooler – and firmer – transfer them to a wire rack to cool completely.

You can make the filling next. Melt the chocolate in a microwave or in a bain-marie and then spread a little of the chocolate over the flat side of half the biscuits. Make a sandwich by sticking the remaining biscuits to the chocolate.

Chocolate kisses

Substitute 4 tablespoons of the flour with 4 tablespoons of cocoa powder, and the almonds with the same quantity of hazelnuts. The hazelnuts do not need the preliminary toasting in the oven nor do you need to peel them. We fill these kisses with butter icing with added deep-red food colouring.

Pistachio kisses

These just happened by accident when I made some kisses with ground pistachio nuts instead of almonds. On seeing the biscuits speckled with green, Johnny commented that they looked like the cheeks of a dying lady, and he didn't want any kisses! But they tasted very good and I decided that the filling should be white butter icing (see p.225), tinged with a little green food colouring to make them even more gruesome. Many children seem to love such macabre images.

Ricotta cake

A few years ago, Sainsbury's asked me to write a piece for their magazine to celebrate Mother's Day, which, that particular year, the food editor decided was going to be Grandmother's Day. I was the lucky grandmother. I had to write 5 recipes for dishes that my grandchildren loved and were going to eat on Mother's Day. We discussed the dishes they would like me to make and, to a certain extent, we chose them together.

The day of the photo shoot arrived with my grandchildren, all clean and polished, on their best behaviour. It went extremely well, the food was delicious, the photos were superb and we had an amazing day. Johnny, who was then 10, declared that the lunch was the best meal he'd ever had.

This is the pudding I made, which on that day I served with Caramelised Oranges (see p.114), one of the fruits in season in March, when Mother's Day occurs. I am an old-fashioned cook who still prefers to use seasonal ingredients, so if Mother's Day were to fall in late spring, I would have chosen the Poached Blueberries on p.60, or a bowl of raspberries or strawberries to accompany the cake. When I use strawberries, I cut them in halves, or even quarters if large, put them in a bowl, and dress them with some lemon juice and a tablespoon or two of caster sugar. I add the lemon juice and the sugar to draw out their juice, which is needed here to moisten the cake.

Serves 6–8

250g golden caster sugar,
    plus 1 tbsp
125g unsalted butter, softened,
    plus more for greasing
4 organic eggs
1kg ricotta
grated rind of 1 organic lemon
75g potato flour, sifted
1 tbsp baking powder
pinch of salt
icing sugar, for dusting
    (optional)

Preheat the oven to 180°C/gas mark 4.

Beat the 250g sugar and the butter together in a bowl until the mixture is light and creamy. After that beat in the eggs, one at a time, and then incorporate the ricotta thoroughly. When the mixture is smooth, mix in the lemon rind, potato flour, baking powder and a pinch of salt. Mix thoroughly again.

Line a 23cm springform cake tin with baking parchment and grease the paper with a little butter. Sprinkle with the remaining 1 tablespoon sugar and then spoon in the ricotta mixture. Bake for 1–1¼ hours until the cake is cooked through. A cocktail stick inserted into the middle of the cake should come out clean when the cake is ready. Leave the cake to cool completely in the tin and then release it onto a dish. Dust with icing sugar, if you want. I find children love doing this.

Caramelised oranges

This is the orange salad I served at that unforgettable Mother's Day photo shoot lunch to accompany the ricotta cake on p.113.

In my experience, even children who are not keen on oranges love them when they are prepared in this way. I prefer oranges that are not too sweet; they should have that characteristic citrussy acidity.

This is the sort of dish that can be made only by an older child who is quite familiar with the different processes of cooking and knows how important it is to be careful with very hot sugar.

Serves 6–8, depending on the size of the oranges

8 organic oranges
225g caster sugar
4 tbsp lemon juice
150ml boiling water

Wash 3 of the oranges and remove their peel, but none of the pith. I use a potato peeler and it is easy.

Bring a small saucepan of water to the boil. Cut the peel into matchsticks, plunge them into the boiling water and boil for 5 minutes to rid them of their bitterness. Drain and set aside.

Peel and remove the skin and pith from all the remaining oranges, and the pith from the 3 used earlier, slice them thinly and put them in a bowl. Put the sugar, lemon juice and 2 tablespoons of water in a small saucepan to make a caramel. Do not stir the syrup; let it cook over a medium heat until golden, which will take about 15 minutes. Now mix in 150ml boiling water – be careful not to have your Coco too close because the syrup might splutter a bit – and then add the matchsticks of peel. Cook for 5 minutes and then leave to cool before pouring it over the orange slices. Cover the bowl with clingfilm and chill before serving.

Pavlovine

Mini pavlovas

Some 40 years ago my god-daughter Sarah made for me what I thought was the best pavlova I have ever eaten. Now that I have eaten many more pavlovas, I still think that her recipe is one of the best and I still use it. What I have often done with my grandchildren is make mini pavlovas so that they can choose their own toppings. Soft berries, passion fruit and poached peaches are all good. I might try Caramelised Oranges (p.114) next time. This is a real treat for them. I know what Coco's favourite is: raspberries and just the thinnest layer of cream.

Makes 10 mini pavlovas
whites of 4 organic eggs,
    at room temperature
250g caster sugar
1 tbsp cornflour
1 tsp vinegar
300ml double cream

Preheat the oven to 200°C/gas mark 6.

Put the egg whites in a large, clean bowl and whisk until they hold stiff peaks. The whites should be so stiff that you could turn the bowl upside down over your head without being covered with meringue. Whisk in half the sugar, and go on whisking until it is very stiff and glossy. Continue whisking and adding sugar, 1 tablespoon at a time. Then beat in the cornflour and the vinegar.

Line 1 or 2 baking sheets with parchment paper and then draw 10 circles, each about 8cm in diameter. Pipe or spoon the meringue mixture equally on the circles – about 2½ tablespoons per circle – smoothing it around with a spatula. With the back of a spoon make a hollow in the middle of each mound. Put the tray in the oven and turn the heat down to 130°C/gas mark ½. Bake for 1 hour and 15 minutes and then turn the oven off and let the *pavlovine* cool completely in the oven.

Whip the cream and, when the *pavlovine* are cold, spread some over each one and pile on the chosen fruit.

Raspberry granita

Frankly, I don't think Coco or any of the children I know like making granita; but they certainly like eating it. As with ice-cream, there is not much amusement in the actual preparation; the fun is in the anticipation of the pleasure to come later.

When she was younger, I managed to get Coco into the kitchen to make this raspberry granita, simply because she had to help me with gathering the fruit. Being small and supple, she could squeeze through the fruit cage and get all the berries on the low branches that I always find impossible to pick.

In the kitchen, the fun was limited to stealing and eating as many berries as she could without my seeing her.

Serves 6
400g raspberries
200g caster sugar
400ml water
juice of 1 lemon

Put the berries into a round fine sieve, set on a bowl, and push them through with a spoon until only the hard bits are left on the sieve. (As Coco grew older, I could bribe her to do some of this boring sieving by letting her eat some of the berries.)

Put the sugar in a saucepan and add the 400ml water. Bring this slowly to the boil and then simmer until the sugar is dissolved, stirring the whole time. Mix in the lemon juice and then let the syrup cool down.

When cold, pour the syrup over the raspberry purée in the bowl and mix thoroughly. Take a metal container, the shallower the better (a frying pan with a removable handle is ideal, but not a non-stick one) and spoon the purée into it. Place the container in the freezer and leave for an hour or so. After that, beat the purée energetically with a fork to break up all the crystals. Leave the granita in the freezer for at least 4 hours, beating it with a fork every 20 minutes or so.

Put the granita in the fridge for some 20 minutes before you want to eat it. It is far nicer when the crystals are not too solid.

3
Inventing & Creating

I remember that it was when she was about 9 years old that Coco began to assert her personality in the cooking we did together. She still needed a lot of advice and guidance, but she was also prepared to suggest little changes and to give her cooking her own mark. She was so very proud when one day she produced a smoothie that I had no idea she had been making.

At around this age, Coco's favourite dishes were any that could be turned over and then appear in a different guise, like the Upside-down sausage and onion tart on p.150. Coco loved the surprise look of the finished dish.

Cheese on toast

alias *Welsh rabbit*

I still remember when I first came across the name of this snack. It was some 50 years ago when one of my sons came back from school and told me that they had had a very good dish for lunch called Welsh rabbit.

'I am sure you liked it; you like rabbit.'

'Oh, but there was no rabbit in it.'

Odd, but true, just as there is no turtle in mock-turtle soup and no duck in Bombay duck. Back then I thought the British were very strange as far as food was concerned, but in spite of that I looked up Welsh rabbit in Constance Spry's book and started making it. It was easy and nutritious and I could find all the ingredients in any good shop nearby.

When I started making this for Coco's tea, there was no problem in finding the right ingredients in any shop. Occasionally we replace some of the Cheddar with Gruyère, which she loves, sometimes with Parmesan, which I love; but fundamentally it is the Cheddar that makes or breaks a good Welsh rabbit (not rarebit, by the way, that name is a later corruption). I use Montgomery's or Quickes' Cheddar, strong and full of pasture flavour.

Coco now makes cheese on toast by herself. Sometimes she adds her favourite touch, by spreading a little anchovy paste on the toasted bread before adding the cheese mixture, as Constance Spry suggests. Other times she makes Johnny's favourite, by laying a slice of smoked ham on the toast and then piling on the cheese mixture. But fundamentally she sticks to Constance Spry's recipe for what Spry calls 'Quick Rabbit', which – she writes – 'is not a true Welsh rabbit, but more of a toasted cheese.'

Makes 4 toasts

4 slices good white bread
butter, for spreading on toast
3–4 tbsp full-fat milk
120g mature Cheddar,
    coarsely grated
pinch or 2 of cayenne pepper
freshly ground black pepper,
    to taste

Preheat the grill to a medium heat.

Toast the bread and butter it generously on one side. Put the milk in a saucepan and bring just up to the simmering point; try to catch it before it really boils. Take off the heat, stir in the cheese and season with the 2 peppers. I find that it does not need salt, but you may like to ask your Coco for her opinion. Spread the mixture on the buttered toasts and grill until brown.

Spaghetti in bianco con le vongole

Spaghetti with clams

There are 2 sauces that Coco loves: one is *Amatriciana* (see p.181) and the other is this one with clams. But while we can make *Amatriciana* every week, or even more often, this sauce is not so easy to make, for no better reason than that the true clams – what the French call *palourdes* – are very difficult to find in this country. I live in Dorset, relatively near the coast, and I always wonder why the choice of fish and seafood I see on the fish stalls at any of the local markets is so limited. Where do the real clams found locally go? I expect they go to France and Spain, where people appreciate them. I don't like the common or garden clams and I don't bother to buy them; they don't have enough taste and are often rubbery and full of sand. But whenever I see the *palourdes*, I buy them, take them home and get a delighted Coco into the kitchen with me.

It is in Italy, at the family house in Le Marche, that we gorge on *palourdes* and this is indeed the best way to eat them: on top of a mountain of spaghetti but with no tomatoes, so that the flavour of the clams can come through loud and clear.

Coco helps with the cleaning and washing of the bivalves and checks that they are all closed, i.e. alive, before we cook them. After that, the recipe is so simple that there is not much to do. Just cook a lot of spaghetti and tuck in.

Serves 4–5

1kg clams
100ml dry white wine
400g spaghetti
5 tbsp extra-virgin olive oil
2 garlic cloves, finely chopped
bunch of flat-leaf parsley,
    chopped
1 small dried chilli, seeded
    and chopped
sea salt, to taste

Put the clams into a sink of cold water and, if they are dirty, scrub them with a hard brush. Leave them in the water for 20 minutes or so to disgorge any sand. Throw away any clam that remains open after being tapped on a hard surface. Change the water and rinse them again.

Pour the wine into a large frying pan, add the clams, cover with a lid and put the pan over a high heat for about 3–4 minutes. Shake the pan every now and then. When the clams are open, set aside about 20 of the largest. Remove the meat from the shells of the remaining clams and discard their shells.

If there is sand at the bottom of the pan, strain the liquid through a sieve lined with muslin and set on a bowl. Rinse the pan and pour the strained liquid back into it. But if the liquid looks clean, pour it gently into the bowl so that if there is a tiny bit of sand at the bottom of the pan it will stay there. Rinse the pan and add the clam liquid. Then put the pan over a high heat to reduce the liquid by half. Pour it back into the bowl.

Cook the spaghetti in salted boiling water as usual.

While the spaghetti is cooking, heat the oil with the garlic, parsley and chilli for 2 minutes, using the same large frying pan. When the pasta is done, drain it and turn immediately into the pan. Add the clam juices and stir-fry for 1 minute, then add the clams without the shells and stir-fry for another 2 minutes. Dish out the pasta onto 4 individual plates and scatter the clams in the shells over each mound.

Thai chicken with noodles

A few years ago Coco asked me to cook a Thai dish with her that has the attraction of containing 'Chinese fettuccine', as we call noodles in our house. I realised that all my cooking with her, and also without her for that matter, had been confined to Italy, mainly, and England (or, to be correct, Great Britain), or France. I am pretty sure I know a lot about a large number of ingredients – I do know how best to cook them – but all this knowledge applies mainly to ingredients that are used in Italian cooking, for which you can read European. This is, I am afraid, a failing of most of us Italians. It is not because we don't like the other cuisines; it is because our cuisine is so strong and good and extensive that we tend to stick to it.

So, that day when Coco brought me a recipe cut out of a newspaper, I decided to turn over a new leaf and learn with her to cook a few dishes from India, Thailand, Morocco, the Middle East, or wherever she chose. I wanted Coco to be more open-minded and receptive than I have been and so we learned together. Often I had to give my Italian touch to whatever I was cooking and I hope it was an improvement; it was at least my signature.

This was indeed the first foreign dish we made together, a dish that has been changed and 'improved' through the years. Now I feel it is totally 'ours', and I cannot remember what we adapted.

Serves 4

300ml coconut cream
2 tbsp Thai red curry paste
3 garlic cloves, crushed
3cm piece fresh ginger, peeled
    and finely chopped
juice of 2 limes
pinch of salt
4 organic chicken breasts,
    boned and skinned
2 tbsp vegetable oil
250g frozen peas, defrosted
300g medium egg noodles
a few sprigs fresh coriander,
    chopped

Take a large bowl and put into it the coconut cream, Thai paste, garlic, ginger, half the lime juice and a pinch of salt. Mix well with a fork.

Cut the chicken breasts into thin slices and mix well into the marinade. Leave for an hour or so.

Pour the oil into a frying pan, add the chicken with all its marinade and stir thoroughly. Cover the pan and cook over a gentle heat for 5 minutes. Add the peas and continue cooking until the peas are tender, about 5 minutes.

Meanwhile, cook the noodles in boiling water, following the instructions on the pack. Drain and turn the noodles into the frying pan. Then stir-fry for 2 or 3 minutes until everything is well mixed together. Mix in the remaining lime juice, taste, adjust the seasoning and sprinkle with the fresh coriander before serving.

Gnocchi di patate

Potato gnocchi

My grandchildren enjoy making all kinds of gnocchi but, given the choice, they always opt for potato gnocchi. We also make choux pastry gnocchi, butternut squash gnocchi, spinach gnocchi, semolina gnocchi, polenta gnocchi, ricotta gnocchi and milk gnocchi. But the favourite by far remains the potato gnocchi, followed by the sweet and comforting *gnocchi di latte*, milk gnocchi (see p.58).

I decided to include 2 recipes in this book and after much thought and consultation with Coco we decided on potato gnocchi and sweet milk gnocchi (see p.58), the first rather difficult and laborious, but great fun to make, the second easier and quicker.

Whenever I make potato gnocchi with my grandchildren, I am taken back some 70 years to our kitchen in Milan, where I spent all the time I could with Maria, our beloved cook, who made legendary potato gnocchi, which my brother Marco still raves about – and so do I. I used to make the rolls, cut and flip the gnocchi and she used to say '*Bravissima*! You are better than me.' I am neither as good at making gnocchi nor as patient with Coco and her siblings as Maria was with me. Sometimes I feel lazy and decide to skip the flipping, which can take a long time; Coco complains and says that they are not proper gnocchi and she is right. 'Just like those in any supermarket' – the final insult. Other times, if I eliminate the flipping, I let Coco do the 'dimpling' (pressing her thumb on each *gnocco* to make a small hollow), which is far quicker than flipping.

Serves 4

1kg old floury potatoes,
    all the same size, if possible
200g Italian 00 flour
1½ tsp sea salt, plus 1 tbsp

Wash the potatoes and boil them in their skins. When they are just soft, but certainly not broken, drain and peel them. It is far easier to peel them when they are still hot, as long as you put on some rubber gloves, of course. Now that Coco is 12, she reluctantly helps me with the peeling. I give her a pair of those surgical (vinyl) gloves and off we go. After that we purée the potatoes through a food mill, which she likes turning. She finds the potato ricer is far too hard to squeeze. We purée them straight onto the work surface and spread them out a little so that they cool faster. Potatoes absorb less flour when cold and the less flour gnocchi contain the better they are.

Then put the flour on the work surface next to the potatoes and gradually mix about three-quarters of the flour and the 1½ teaspoons of salt into the potatoes. I knead (now Coco kneads) and, if too wet, we add a little more flour. It is impossible to say how much flour you will need to add. It all depends on the variety of the potatoes and also on the temperature and humidity of the room. The dough is ready when you can gather it all up into a sticky but beautifully smooth ball. Wrap the ball in clingfilm and leave it in the fridge for an hour or two. It is far easier to make gnocchi with a chilled dough.

Next take the ball out of the fridge and pile some flour in a corner of the work surface. Now the fun starts for the children. Pinch out a good fistful of dough and, with floured hands, roll it out on the work surface to make a long sausage, about 2cm thick. Cut the sausage into 2cm pieces and spread them out on tea towels, keeping them slightly separate. The gnocchi are now ready to be cooked as they are, or they can be grooved or dimpled.

To groove, lightly press each *gnocco* against the floured tines of a fork. You can do this either up the tines, or down the tines as we do. Let them fall back onto the tea towels. By the way, the grooves are not put there for decoration; they are there to hold more sauce and make the gnocchi more tasty. The same applies to the dimples, which are made by simply pressing a floured thumb or an index finger onto each little dumpling. 'Just like having your fingerprints taken,' my grandson Johnny commented when he first did it.

Now take out a shallow oven dish into which you can put the gnocchi once they are cooked, and butter it all over.

To cook the gnocchi, bring a large pan of water to the boil and add the 1 tablespoon salt. Don't throw them all in at the same time as they might stick together, but cook them in 2 or even 3 batches, depending on the size of your pan. At first the gnocchi will sink to the bottom of the pan but then they will come up to the surface. Coco counts up to 20 and then 'I rescue them!' she screams, brandishing my *schiumarola*, an invaluable Italian tool similar to a large and flat slotted spoon. While she 'rescues' the gnocchi and puts them in the buttered dish, I dry them slightly with some kitchen paper. When they are 'rescued' they are dressed with whatever sauce we have chosen. The children love them with pesto, I prefer them with butter melted in a small saucepan with 2 cloves of squashed garlic (which I remove before using it) and a dozen fresh, torn-up sage leaves, all sautéed together to a golden colour. But they are equally delicious with a simple tomato sauce (see p.34) or with a good lump of Gorgonzola melted in some double cream. When the potatoes are of a good quality, gnocchi are food for the gods that any mortal can afford.

Baked polenta
with mushrooms and cheese

Three winters ago we went skiing, which actually means that they, the family, skied while I looked after little Kate. The weather was perfect and I spent the mornings sitting in the sun watching her throw herself down the children's slope and then taking her to have hot chocolate and a slice of strudel in the café in the square of the village in the Dolomites, where we were staying.

One day Coco arrived back at the hotel flushed with excitement: 'Nonna, Nonna! You must come up tomorrow for lunch to eat the polenta I had today at the *rifugio* (refuge).'

'But, Coco, you don't like polenta,' I answered.

'Oh yes I do, when it's like that.'

The next day, come 12 o'clock, Kate and I took the ski-lift and were carried up high through the peaks to meet Coco and the others for lunch. Among the array of pastas and *risotti* and sausages and potatoes and polenta, Coco quickly spotted her favourite tray and asked the girl behind the counter for 2 portions, in perfect Italian (I was delighted to see that when she wants to communicate, she can do it very well in a language that she claims she does not understand). We sat outside in the blazing sun, I tasted the polenta and said, 'But Coco, I make this too and the recipe is in one of my books.' 'Oh, Nonna, then we can make it at home.'

Back home, we did but, of course, it didn't taste so good. The gentle hills of Dorset could not compete with the majestic peaks of the Dolomites, nor the pale winter light of England with the radiant sunshine in the Alps. Also our baked polenta was a gentler version of the original. It missed the wild porcini, and the polenta itself – which here we had to make with the more easily available flour, the instant polenta – did not have that deep flavour that a polenta made with the local maize has. Still, we all enjoyed it and here is the recipe. I often make the dish in the autumn, using mushrooms that we pick ourselves: *boleti* and other kinds, all mixed up. But you can make it all through the winter with cultivated mushrooms and dried porcini and it is equally delicious.

Make the polenta, following the packet instructions, some 3 hours in advance – a job I suggest you do on your own, because it is hardly a thrilling task for any child. When the polenta is cooked, spoon it onto a board and flatten it out to a thickness of about 2cm,

Serves 6

polenta made with 300g
    polenta flour
6 tbsp full-fat milk
20g dried porcini mushrooms
béchamel sauce made with
    500ml full-fat milk,
    60g unsalted butter and
    50g Italian 00 flour
250g cultivated mushrooms
    (e.g. chestnut mushrooms,
    field mushrooms, oyster
    mushrooms), cleaned and
    sliced
15g unsalted butter
3 tbsp olive oil
1 garlic clove, finely chopped
grating of nutmeg
40g Gruyère
40g mature Cheddar
40g Manchego or pecorino
6 tbsp freshly grated
    Parmigiano-Reggiano
sea salt and freshly ground
    black pepper, to taste
butter, for greasing

using a wet spatula. Your Coco might be willing to do that. (You must make it at least 3 hours in advance, but you can also make it 1 or 2 days in advance and chill it.)

Bring the 6 tablespoons milk to the boil and pour it over the porcini. Leave them to soak, while you make the béchamel. Coco can now make this sauce all on her own and it seldom gets lumpy. She puts the 500ml milk in my Italian milk boiler (a sort of tall pan) and puts it on a very low heat. She puts the 60g butter in a saucepan and, when it is melted and just beginning to sizzle, she removes the pan from the heat and adds the 50g flour, while with the other hand she beats hard with a wooden spoon. She puts the pan back on the heat and cooks, beating for 1 minute, and then she begins, very gradually, to add the hot milk, which by then has just reached the right temperature, nearly boiling point. She beats and beats and beats while she pours in the milk. (I must admit that occasionally the béchamel goes lumpy and then, practically in tears, she asks me to come to the rescue. Easy – I give it a blast in the food processor.) She lets the sauce boil gently for 2 or 3 minutes and then she adds a little salt and turns to cooking the mushrooms, one of her favourite foods.

To prepare the mushrooms, wipe them clean with some kitchen paper and slice them. If the caps are too large, cut them in half. Put the butter, oil and the garlic in a large frying pan and put it on the heat, while fishing the porcini out of the milk and chopping them roughly. Reserve the milk. When the fats in the frying pan are hot throw in the porcini and sauté them for 3 minutes, followed by the cultivated mushrooms. Season with nutmeg and salt and pepper and sauté for a few minutes more over a high heat, stirring the whole time. The mushrooms will release their liquid. Now it's time to add the milk in which the porcini were soaking. Add it very slowly so that, if the porcini have deposited some grit, it will stay at the bottom of the bowl. Let the mushrooms cook for about 10 minutes. Check that there is always enough liquid in the pan; if it gets too dry add some hot water.

While the mushrooms are cooking, slice the cheeses and preheat the oven to 180°C/gas mark 4.

The assembly of the dish is fun. Cut the polenta into large strips. Butter a lasagne dish that measures 20 x 16cm and spread 2 or 3 tablespoons of béchamel sauce over the bottom. Lay about a third of the polenta slices over this and cover with half the mushrooms, half the sliced cheeses, a couple of tablespoons of Parmesan and the same of béchamel. Then cover with another layer of polenta. Repeat all these layers and finish with a layer of polenta, which should be covered all over with the remaining béchamel and sprinkled with what is left of the grated Parmesan. Place the dish in the oven for at least 30 minutes.

Bring the dish to the table some 5 minutes after it has come out of the oven and enjoy it when it is not piping hot. You will love it – even without memories of a wonderful skiing holiday to go with it.

You can make a delicious lasagne dish with the same layers.

Chicken stuffed with bread sauce

I love bread sauce – something totally English that I have absorbed into my culinary repertoire. So my children and grandchildren have always had it when I roast a chicken in the oven à l'anglaise.

A few years ago Coco, who often comes into my kitchen to see what I am cooking, said: 'But, Nonna, why don't we try to cook the bread sauce together with the chicken? We can just put it up its bum.' And so we did. It was a great success.

Serves 6
120–150g stale white bread, crustless weight
½ medium-sized onion, cut into pieces
about 300ml full-fat milk
1 organic chicken, approx 1.5kg
3 pinches ground cloves
generous grating of nutmeg
50g unsalted butter, at room temperature
2 garlic cloves, crushed
2–3 sprigs fresh rosemary
1 tbsp olive oil
150ml dry white wine
sea salt and freshly ground black pepper, to taste

Preheat the oven to 150°C/gas mark 2.

Tear the bread into small chunks. Spread it onto a baking tray and put it into the oven for about 10 minutes to dry out. Now turn up the oven to 200°C/gas mark 6. Put the bread pieces into the food processor, together with the onion, and whiz it until it's all crumby. Scoop this into a bowl, add enough milk to cover the bread and leave it while you prepare the bird.

Wipe the chicken inside and out with kitchen paper and season it with salt and pepper. Now go back to the bread and squeeze out all the milk. Season the bread with salt and pepper and with the spices and half the butter, cut into tiny pieces. Coco makes a sort of paste with her hands and pushes the stuffing 'up the bum!' of the chicken while I hold it bottom up to make it easier for her. Stitch up the skin with 2 cocktail sticks all around the hole and place it in a roasting tin ready to be cooked. Then smear the rest of the butter all over the bird and add the garlic, rosemary, oil and wine. Place the tin in the oven for about 1¼ hours, turning the chicken over once and basting it 2 or 3 times. To check if it is cooked, cut into the flesh between the body and the thigh. The juices should run clear. You should also make sure that the stuffing is piping hot right through.

After you've turned off the heat, leave the chicken in the oven for about 15 minutes to relax the flesh. I never make a gravy, because the winey juices are quite enough.

Polpettone *Meatloaf*

Polpettone is the large version of *polpette* (meatballs, see p.43), as its name implies. But it is a more difficult dish to prepare than its smaller cousins. For this reason I didn't start making it with Coco until she was older; I didn't want to put her off making a dish that I like and which is a godsend for using up leftovers, although you can use fresh mince. I don't know why but I tend to make *polpettone* mostly with leftover roast meat, a trend which I might have started at Christmas time urged by the sight of endless turkey.

This is how I taught Coco to make a good *polpettone* with leftover roast meat – beef, turkey, chicken or pork, but not lamb – but you can use fresh beef or pork mince or, better still, a mixture of the two.

Serves 5–6

500g leftover roast meat
100g mortadella
4 organic eggs
100g Parmigiano-Reggiano, freshly grated
100–125g dried white bread-crumbs (see p.12)
4 tbsp chopped flat-leaf parsley
1 garlic clove, chopped
4 tbsp olive oil
2 sprigs fresh rosemary
15g unsalted butter, at room temperature
1 tbsp Italian 00 flour
100ml dry white wine
150ml beef stock (see p.20)
sea salt and freshly ground black pepper, to taste

Mince the meat and the mortadella together in a food processor, being careful to stop whizzing before it becomes a paste. After that, spoon the mixture into a bowl. Now the fun starts for your Coco with the adding and the mixing and then the shaping. Add 3 whole eggs and the yolk of the fourth, which Coco loves to separate (reserve the white), plus the Parmesan, 75g of the breadcrumbs, the parsley and garlic, and mix and mix into a uniform mass with all available hands. Now it is time for your Coco to taste and add salt, if necessary, and pepper.

Turn the bowl upside down on a board and the whole lot will fall out. Start to work by patting and shaping and patting and shaping the mixture into a large sausage – about 7–8 cm in diameter. It is quite important to pat the roll thoroughly so that any air bubbles come out. When it looks pretty solid, Coco brushes it all over with the reserved egg white and then we roll it in the remaining breadcrumbs, patting them down firmly. Place it in the fridge for at least half an hour.

Preheat the oven to 200°C/gas mark 6.

Spoon the olive oil into a roasting tin and place the tin in the oven. When the oven has reached the right temperature, transfer the roll into the tin, add the rosemary and roast for 1 hour. Lift the roll out of the tin – not easy, I admit, I use one of those invaluable fish slices which opens out like a fan – and put the roll on a board, covering it with a piece of foil to keep warm. If you find it easier, cut the roll in half before you lift it out of the tin.

Now make the sauce. First combine the butter and flour with a fork, to form a paste. Strain the cooking juices from the roasting tin into a small saucepan. Add the wine to the juices and boil it for 1 minute and then add the stock and the flour and butter paste. After a minute or two of gentle boiling, the sauce is ready to be spooned around the sliced *polpettone*.

Coco prefers her *polpettone* served with the mushroom sauce below, which now, aged 12, she makes herself. It goes very well.

Mushroom sauce

20g dried porcini
200ml hot water
2 tbsp olive oil
30g unsalted butter
1 garlic clove, chopped
4 tbsp chopped flat-leaf parsley
250g cultivated mushrooms,
    roughly chopped
1 tsp plain flour
4 tbsp dry sherry
4 tbsp vegetable or chicken
    stock
generous grating of nutmeg
sea salt and freshly ground
    black pepper, to taste

Soak the dried porcini in the hot water for about 20 minutes. Drain, keeping the liquid, and, if there are some large pieces, chop them roughly. Heat the oil and butter in a frying pan, add the garlic and half the parsley and, after 1 minute, throw in the porcini. Cook, stirring, for 2 minutes and then add the mushrooms. Keep over a high heat for 4–5 minutes, stirring frequently. Mix in the flour and, after 1 minute, add the sherry. Let it bubble away for 1 minute and then add the liquid of the porcini, pouring it gently into the pan in case there is sediment at the bottom that must be thrown away. Bring to the boil and add the stock, the nutmeg and the seasoning. Cook the sauce very slowly for 7–8 minutes. Mix in the remaining parsley and serve with the sliced *polpettone*.

Beefy rolls

This is one of the recipes I used to make in order to entice my son Guy to eat vegetables. He loved making these rolls so much that I was able to bribe him to eat them.

Now, 40 years later, I make the same dish with Coco, and Johnny, another very unwilling vegetable eater; he forgets about the spinach because he likes the surrounding meat and gravy so much. If you have a helpful butcher – a must, in my opinion – ask him to cut 8 thin slices from a joint of topside. The same thin steaks can be cut from a piece of rump or from a fillet. You can also find thin steaks in some supermarkets, the easiest option.

Serves 4

8 thin steak slices, about 450g
2 organic eggs
15g Italian 00 flour
100ml full-fat milk
40g Parmigiano-Reggiano,
    freshly grated
4 tbsp olive oil
400g spinach
75g unsalted butter
2 garlic cloves, squashed
3–4 tbsp plain flour
100ml red wine
sea salt and freshly ground
    black pepper, to taste

Take the steaks out of the fridge, put them on a board and, if they're not very thin, get a cleaver or rolling pin and beat them a little to flatten them (you can put the steaks between 2 sheets of greaseproof paper). Then put them aside while you make the eggy pancake. Lightly beat the eggs together in a small bowl and slowly add the flour, milk, Parmesan and some black pepper. Don't add salt because the cheese is already salty enough.

Put 1 tablespoon of the oil in a 20cm non-stick pan and heat it. When hot, pour in half the egg mixture to cover the bottom of the pan. Cook one side, and then flip the pancake over and cook the other side. Do the same with the other half of the egg mixture. Set the 2 pancakes aside to cool.

Pick over and wash the spinach in plenty of water. Put it straight into a pan without any water (the water clinging to the leaves is quite enough) and with 1 teaspoon salt. Place the pan over a high heat and cook for about 2 minutes, turning the spinach over and over. Drain very thoroughly and squeeze out all the water with your hands as soon as the spinach is cool enough. Put the spinach on a board and chop roughly by hand, not in a food processor which would reduce it to a purée. Heat half the butter in a frying pan, throw in the garlic and cook for 1 minute. Add the spinach and cook for about 3 minutes, turning it over often. Fish out the garlic and discard it.

Now everything is ready for your Coco to get to work. Lightly sprinkle the steaks with salt and pepper. Cut out 8 pieces of pancake just a little smaller than the steaks and lay a piece over each steak. Spread a layer of spinach over each piece, leaving a small clean edge all around. Roll up each steak and stitch with a wooden cocktail stick (Coco's speciality). Coat the bundles very lightly in the plain flour seasoned with ½ teaspoon salt, and they are now ready to be cooked.

Heat the remaining butter and oil in a large frying pan and, when the fat is sizzling, slide in the rolls. Cook them for 4 minutes until they are brown all over and then pour over the wine and let it bubble away for 2 minutes or so. Turn the heat down, add 2–3 tablespoons water and cook for a further 3 minutes. Lift the bundles out of the pan and keep them warm in a low oven while you finish off the cooking juices by adding a few more tablespoons of boiling water. Boil rapidly and let the juices reduce until they are syrupy. Spoon the juices over the bundles and serve straight away.

Fish cakes

Fish fingers and fish cakes are often the only way children will eat fish. They like the crust and forget about what's inside. Fish cakes are also fun to make and any child is usually willing to help in the preparation. And if they are willing to help, they should also be willing to eat the result of their efforts.

Serves 4

300g floury potatoes, peeled
    and cut into chunks
300g white fish, such as cod,
    pollock or coley
½ onion, with skin left on
2 bay leaves
15g capers
½ garlic clove
20g flat-leaf parsley
25g unsalted butter
grated rind and juice of
    ½ organic lemon
50g fresh breadcrumbs
    (see p.13)
vegetable oil, for frying
sea salt and freshly ground
    black pepper, to taste

Boil the potatoes in slightly salted water until soft. While the potatoes are cooking, wash the fish and lay it in a saucepan. Add the onion, bay leaves and a pinch of salt and cover with cold water. Bring slowly to the boil and then turn the heat off and leave the fish in the liquid to cool, while you chop the capers, garlic and parsley together.

When the potatoes are cooked, drain and mash them with a potato ricer or a masher. Add the butter and a little salt and beat well. It does not matter if there are some small lumps. When the fish is cool, lift it out of the liquid and remove the skin and any bones. Break up the fish with a fork into smallish pieces and put into a bowl. Add the mashed potatoes, the chopped ingredients, lemon juice and rind, the breadcrumbs and black pepper to taste and mix everything together.

Now you are ready to shape the fish cakes, a job which, I am sure, your Coco will like, as mine does. First ask her to taste the mixture and check if the salt and pepper and lemon juice are right. Then roughly divide the mixture into 8 portions. Pick up a portion at a time and shape it in your hands. I shape them not so much as round balls but as flattened-out balls, like thick hamburgers. This is because you need less oil to fry them. If you moisten your hands with water you will find it easier to make the shapes, since the mixture will not stick easily to them.

Pour some oil into a large frying pan or a wok to come about 1.5cm up the sides of the pan. When the oil is very hot, but not yet smoking, slide in the fish cakes and cook them for about 5 minutes until a lovely golden crust has formed. Turn them over gently with a fish slice and cook the other side. When the underside is also golden, put them on the plates and enjoy.

I like them with a squeeze of lemon juice, while my grandchildren, I am ashamed to admit it, have them with their beloved tomato ketchup.

Peperonata *Pepper ratatouille*

Coco has always liked vegetables, cooked and raw alike, and this is one of her favourite vegetable dishes. I wonder if she likes it because she used to enjoy helping to cut the peppers into strips ('not too wide, but not too thin,' I would tell her) and then mixing them all together before chucking them into the pan of sautéed onion, whose smell pervades the whole kitchen. Most of all she loves leftover *peperonata*, with which I make her favourite frittata (p.154). So, with the frittata in mind, I always make more *peperonata* than needed – it is also excellent for dressing a plateful of spaghetti the next day.

I have learned from Coco to add balsamic vinegar instead of wine vinegar. Coco adores the balsamic type and whenever vinegar is needed, she asks for it. And now I do think *peperonata* is better with balsamic vinegar because its sweetness tempers the capsicum flavour.

Serves 4

4 sweet peppers, of mixed colours
1– 2 red chillies (optional)
75ml extra-virgin olive oil
2 large red onions, finely sliced
400g ripe tomatoes, peeled, seeded and roughly chopped
2 tbsp balsamic vinegar
2 tbsp chopped flat-leaf parsley
sea salt and freshly ground black pepper, to taste

Wash the peppers, cut them into quarters and remove and discard the seeds, cores and ribs. Cut the peppers into strips about 2–2.5cm wide. Cut the chillies in half (if using), scrape off the seeds and cut them into smallish pieces.

Heat the oil in a large sauté or frying pan and throw in the onion. Sauté for 5 minutes and then add the peppers and chillies. Cook for another 5 minutes, stirring so that the peppers are all mixed up with the onion, then add the tomatoes and season with salt and black pepper. Mix well and cook over a moderate heat for about 30 minutes. You might have to add a tablespoon or two of hot water. *Peperonata* should have a little liquid left at the end of the cooking. After that, add the balsamic vinegar and parsley and cook for a further 5 minutes or so.

Call your Coco and ask her to check the seasoning and also whether it's ready. You might like your peppers a bit softer; if so, cook the dish for a little longer. You can eat it hot or cold. Coco and I like it at room temperature.

Roasted-vegetable tart

In my experience most children do not like vegetables; I correct myself, they don't like vegetables just steamed or boiled and then served plain. But as soon as you sauté them with garlic or onion, or braise them with a touch of onion, or stew them with a little tomato purée, or roast them, or mash them with plenty of butter, or stuff them or make a pasta sauce with them or serve them with couscous, they eat them and even tell you how good they are.

This is one of my grandchildren's favourite tarts, which they occasionally ask me to make for them, just 'like Mummy does'. The snag is that Mummy is far better at making pastry than Nonna is. Pastry is not in my cookery repertoire, as indeed it is not in most Italian cooks' repertoires. But living in this country of pastry makers and pastry lovers I had to learn to make it, although it's never a great success. This is my daughter Julia's recipe.

Serves 8

For the pastry:
120g Italian 00 flour
60g unsalted butter, cut into
    small pieces
2 pinches sea salt
1 organic egg, slightly beaten

For the filling:
3 small red onions, sliced
½ medium aubergine, cut into
    small cubes of about 1cm
1 small sweet potato, cut into
    same-sized cubes
1 small courgette, cut into
    same-sized cubes
2 tbsp olive oil
5 organic eggs
125ml double cream
150g goat's cheese (optional)
sea salt and freshly ground
    black pepper, to taste

Preheat the oven to 180°C/gas mark 4.

First make the pastry. To be honest, I never make pastry; my food processor does it. So I have never made it with Coco, but she makes it with her mother (although not very often, I have been told, because Julia also uses the processor). Put the flour in the food processor with the butter on top, and the salt. Whiz for a few seconds, until it's crumbly, and then add enough egg for the pastry to come together. Take the dough out and roll it into a ball. Easy and quick. If you prefer to make the pastry by hand, rub the butter into the flour until it looks like coarse breadcrumbs and then add enough egg to bring it all together into a ball.

Line a 25cm tart tin with the pastry. Place the tin in the fridge for half an hour. Then take the tin out of the fridge, line the uncooked tart with foil or parchment paper and weight it down with uncooked beans or rice. Bake blind for 20 minutes, and then remove the foil or parchment paper and the beans and put the tin back in the oven for 5 minutes so that the bottom of the tart can get golden too.

Now make the filling. Spread the cut vegetables on a baking tray, pour the oil over them and sprinkle with salt and pepper. Mix them up with your hands until the cubes are coated in oil and then place the tray in the hot oven. Coco and Kate love cutting vegetables, cubing more than slicing because it is easier, and then they like mixing up all the veg in the oil. The vegetables will be cooked in about an hour. Taste them after 45 minutes to see if they are ready.

Whisk the eggs into the cream until properly blended and then stir in all the cooked vegetables. Turn the oven up to 190°C/gas mark 5 and place the tart in it. Bake for 20–25 minutes, until the custard is set and firm. If you are using the goat's cheese, put little lumps of it all over the top halfway through the cooking. I love this tart at room temperature.

Squash cups filled with orzotto

I have discovered that all children like squash as well as pumpkin, and I mean eating them as well as carving them up for Halloween. As for me, I don't like pumpkins because of their total lack of flavour. But I love squash and so does Coco. When we started making these squash cups, we used leftover risotto for the filling; then I enjoyed Nigella Lawson's 'Orzotto with Squash' – which she describes in her excellent Christmas book – so much that I suggested to Coco that we should change the rice for barley (*orzo* in Italian). And it is very good. Added to which, the orzotto is easier to make than risotto because you can add the stock all at once and not by the ladleful. Nigella rightly points out the ideal contrast between the softness of the squash and the nubbliness of the barley.

For this dish you can buy small acorn or onion squash but, after much trial and error, I have decided to use butternut squash with the 'neck' cut off. They work best and are cooked and ready to stuff in half an hour, less than the time it takes to make the orzotto.

Serves 4

4 small butternut squashes
60g unsalted butter
1 small shallot, very finely
     chopped
120–150g pearl barley (*orzo*)
100ml dry white wine
500ml hot vegetable stock
     (see p.20)
2 pinches ground cinnamon
generous grating of nutmeg
6 tbsp freshly grated
     Parmigiano-Reggiano
a few blades fresh chives
sea salt and freshly ground
     black pepper, to taste
oil, for greasing

Preheat the oven to 200°C/gas mark 6.

Cut the 'neck' off each squash (keep them for another dish), scoop out all the seeds from the bottoms and put these 'cups' on an oiled baking tray. Coco loves to dig into the squashes and can do a very good job of cleaning them. Put a small lump of butter into each cup, reserving the remainder, and season with salt and pepper. Place the tray in the oven and bake for 25–35 minutes, until the squashes are just tender when you stick the point of a knife into them.

While the squashes are baking, heat the remaining butter in a saucepan, add the shallot and sweat with a pinch of salt until just turning golden. Throw in the barley, mix well and cook, stirring the whole time, for about 2 or 3 minutes. Turn the heat up, pour in the wine and boil for about 2 minutes. Add about three-quarters of the hot stock, bring to the boil, and then add the spices and cook over a moderate heat until the barley is soft – about 40 minutes. Stir occasionally and add more stock if necessary. At the end mix in the cheese.

Now call back your Coco. Give her a teaspoon and ask her to taste and check the salt and pepper and then to fill the squash cups with the orzotto. Put the cups back in the oven for a further 10 minutes. When they are hot, your Coco can cut the chives' blades in half and stick 2 or 3 into each cup. I hope she will enjoy it as much as Coco does.

Upside-down sausage
and onion tart

This is one of the surprise dishes in this chapter that brings laughter and merriment when it is turned over with a flourish.

Serves 4–5

4 tbsp olive oil
500g best pork sausages
100ml red wine
about 100ml boiling water
2 medium-sized onions, very
    finely sliced
200g ready-to-use puff pastry
sea salt and freshly ground
    black pepper, to taste

Preheat the oven to 200°C/gas mark 6.

Heat 1 tablespoon of the oil in a non-stick frying pan. When the oil is hot, throw in the sausages and fry until they form a dark crust all over. Pour in the wine and continue to cook for a further 5 minutes or so. Turn the heat down and pour in about 100ml boiling water. Simmer until there is hardly any liquid left – another 4 or 5 minutes.

Heat the remaining oil in a sauté pan, throw in the sliced onion and a couple of pinches of salt. Sauté until the onion is golden, not brown, stirring it frequently for 10–15 minutes.

While the onion is cooking, slice the sausages in half lengthwise and arrange them in a 20cm round tart tin in a ring, cutting the half-sausages to fit in the shape of the tin. If there is any juice left in the sausage pan add it to the onion. Taste the onion and check for salt, adding pepper if you want. Now spoon it all around the sausages.

Roll out the pastry thinly on a floured board. Cut in a round about 1cm wider than the tin. Roll the pastry round the rolling pin and then unroll it over the sausages and onion in the tin. Tuck in the edges of the pastry all around and then place the tin in the oven. Bake for 25–30 minutes until the pastry is golden.

To unmould, place a large round dish over the top of the tin. Carefully turn the dish over and let the tart drop onto it.

Nell's
middle eastern aubergines

Nell, my oldest granddaughter, is more gifted at the desk than at the stove. But she too knows about food and enjoys eating well, a prerequisite for all my family. Even my very English son-in-law is now a connoisseur of good food and quite a good cook. Nell has recently developed a passion for the Middle East and I am delighted, because she is getting to know food from other parts of the world, outside England and Italy. This is one of her efforts that she produced a couple of years ago – now a staple even in my kitchen, where dishes other than Italian seldom get a look in.

Serves 4

6 tbsp extra-virgin olive oil
1 large onion, thinly sliced
2 garlic cloves, peeled
1 scant tsp coriander seeds
1 scant tsp cumin seeds
2 aubergines (about 600g),
    sliced
3 tbsp pine nuts
2 tbsp sultanas
¼ preserved lemon, chopped
sea salt and freshly ground
    black pepper, to taste
fresh coriander, coarsely
    chopped, to garnish

Pour half the oil in a frying pan and, when hot, throw in the onion and a pinch of salt and fry gently for about 10 minutes, turning it over often. The onion should just get soft not brown. If necessary, add 1 tablespoon hot water.

While the onion is cooking, grind the garlic, coriander seeds and the cumin seeds in a mortar, the perfect task for your Coco. If you can, teach her to grind properly by pressing the pestle in a rotating movement against the side of the mortar, not against the bottom; this is not so easy to do. Add the mixture to the onion, together with a little salt and a generous grinding of pepper, and fry for 5 minutes or so, frequently turning the whole thing over. Now add the aubergines and the remaining oil and cook for 10 minutes. Mix in the pine nuts, sultanas and preserved lemon and continue cooking until the aubergine is nice and soft. Ask your Coco to check the seasoning. Sprinkle with the fresh coriander and eat it hot, warm or cold, but neither piping hot nor fridge cold.

We often eat these aubergines by themselves as an antipasto, but they are also very good with lamb chops, sausages or any other grilled or fried meat or chicken.

Frittata

Far easier to make than an omelette, frittata is its Italian counterpart. The main differences are that a frittata is firm, round and not folded over, and it is cooked over a low heat. Frittata can be served hot or cold, or anything in-between.

A frittata lends itself to be successfully combined with lots of other ingredients, such as pasta, salami, cheeses and most vegetables, such as sautéed courgette or steamed spinach, or even the forgotten food at the bottom of your fridge. The first recipe here is for a frittata with cheese, which is the simplest of them all, and the first one you can make with your Coco.

Frittata with cheese

You can use mature Cheddar instead of Parmesan, or a mixture of the two, and/or some Gruyère.

Serves 4–5

6 organic eggs
100g Parmigiano-Reggiano or
    Cheddar, freshly grated
40g unsalted butter
sea salt and freshly ground
    black pepper, to taste

Lightly beat the eggs in a bowl, mix in the cheese and salt and pepper to taste, but be careful with the salt, because of the saltiness of the cheese.

Put a 25cm frying pan on the heat and add the butter. When the foam from the butter begins to disappear and the butter becomes a lovely golden colour, pour in the egg mixture. Turn down the heat and cook gently for some 7 minutes, until the mixture is firm and only the top surface is runny. Do not stir the mixture. You want it to settle gently.

While the frittata is cooking, preheat the grill to its highest setting. When the frittata is firm but the top is still runny, put the pan under the grill until the top is just set.

Loosen the frittata all around with a palette knife, put a large dish on the top and turn the pan upside down – the frittata will flop onto the dish. Alternatively, cut it into wedges and put them on individual plates, which is easier and saves on washing-up.

Frittata with onions (my favourite)

To the beaten eggs, I add 2 red onions, thinly sliced, previously sautéed in 2 tablespoons olive oil for 15 minutes. I lift the onion out of the pan with a slotted spoon so that I can leave some of the liquid behind.

Frittata with prawns (Coco's favourite)

To the beaten eggs add 250g prawn tails (the frozen sort, defrosted, are perfect for the job), 2 tablespoons chopped flat-leaf parsley and 1 crushed garlic clove. This frittata is best served hot or warm.

Un fiore di pere

A pear flower

This pudding is another dish beloved by Coco for its 'surprise' appearance, like the Upside-down sausage and onion tart on p.150.

Serves 8–10

100g unsalted butter, at room
    temperature, plus more
    for greasing
120g caster sugar
yolks of 2 organic eggs
140g Italian 00 flour
pinch of salt
2 tsp baking powder
grated zest of 1 organic orange
2 tbsp orange flower water
2 tbsp light brown sugar
1 tsp ground cinnamon
1 dried fig
8 pears, ripe but firm
butter, for greasing

Preheat the oven to 180°C/gas mark 4.

Cream together the butter and the sugar until light. We do this with an electric hand-held whisk, slow to start off and then at higher speed, which is far easier for Coco than doing it by hand. If the butter is not soft enough, the mixture will spatter everywhere – which might be more fun for her but is certainly not for me.

Add the yolks one at a time, then gradually add the flour, salt and baking powder and continue beating until everything is well blended. Mix in the grated orange zest and the orange water.

Lightly butter the bottom of a 25cm springform cake tin. Line it with parchment paper and then butter the paper and the sides very generously. Mix together the brown sugar and the cinnamon and sprinkle half of it over the bottom of the tin. Beat the fig down with the palm of your hand to flatten it and place it in the centre of the tin. Peel the pears, cut into halves and arrange them in the bottom of the tin like 'petals of a daisy'. The fig is the centre of the flower.

Spoon the cake mixture over the pears, put the tin in the oven and bake for 1 hour.

Turn the heat off and sprinkle the cake with the remaining sugar and cinnamon. Leave the tin in the oven for a further 10 minutes, then take it out and loosen the spring clip, but leave the cake in the tin until cold.

Re-clasp the clip and turn the tin upside down over a round dish. The cake will fall out easily and the surprise flower will be there. Serve with pouring cream.

Crema fritta

Custard fritters

This used to be my favourite fritter, which our cook, Maria, made to perfection. She made all fritters to perfection – not an easy task. My *crema fritta* is certainly not as good, although Coco thinks it is delicious and, over the years, has often begged me to make it. We usually make the custard in the morning and then fry the cut-up pieces in the evening, a perfect pud for the children's supper.

Serves 4

For the crème pâtissière
    (pastry cream):
yolks of 3 organic eggs
100g icing sugar, sifted
75g Italian 00 flour
500ml full-fat milk
strip of rind from 1 organic lemon
15g unsalted butter, melted

For the coating:
1 organic egg
130–150g dried white
    breadcrumbs (see p.12)
vegetable oil, for frying
icing sugar, for dusting

Put the egg yolks and icing sugar in a heavy-based saucepan, beat well with a wooden spoon and then gradually add the flour, while beating constantly.

Heat the milk with the strip of lemon rind until just beginning to boil and then pour it over the egg mixture, beating hard the whole time. When all the milk has been incorporated, put the saucepan on the heat and bring it very slowly to the boil. Simmer for 5 minutes, stirring the whole time, to get rid of the unpleasant taste of raw flour. The custard will be quite thick at the end. Remove it from the heat and beat in the melted butter.

Before I continue, I ask Coco to fish out the lemon rind with a metal spoon, so that she can enjoy licking it clean, and then throw it away. Then we moisten a baking tray with cold water and, with a wet spatula, spread the custard over it to a thickness of about 4cm. When cool, place the tray in the fridge. The custard must now get cold, which takes at least 2 hours.

Cut the custard into squares, wide strips or lozenges, or whatever shapes your Coco wants. In a soup bowl, lightly beat the egg. Spread the breadcrumbs on a plate. Lightly coat a piece of custard with some crumbs and then dip it in the egg. Let the surplus egg fall back into the dish before you give the custard a final coating of crumbs, patting them firmly in. Repeat with all the remaining pieces of custard. This is great fun for children but for the next step I prefer Coco to observe, and from a reasonable distance too.

Put a large frying pan on the heat and pour in enough oil to come about 2cm up the sides of the pan. When the oil is very hot, but not smoking, carefully slide in enough custard pieces so that they are quite well spaced. Fry until a golden crust has formed on the bottom, then turn the pieces over and fry the other side until this is golden too. Lift them out with a fish slice and put them on kitchen paper to drain.

Sprinkle lavishly with icing sugar before you bring the dish to the table. *Crema fritta*, like any fritter, should be eaten hot.

Pan di miglio

St George's buns

Two or three years ago on St George's Day, the 23rd of April, I suddenly remembered the biscuits we used to make when I was a child in Milan. In Lombardy, St George is the patron saint of the dairy farmers and these large soft buns are served floating in a pond of thick cream. So on that particular St George's Day, when Coco came back from school, we made these delicious buns. But we had to make a necessary change: we left out the elderflowers, the traditional flavouring of the Milanese originals, because elderflowers are not in bloom in Dorset so early in the year. Instead we decided to add grated lemon zest, which I find such a perfect flavouring. However I suggest you forget St George's Day, and make these buns whenever you can pick elderflowers in full bloom. They have a heavenly scent and they are a good excuse for a picnic in the countryside in June.

You will need to pick a full basket of flowers. When you get back home, get your Coco and any other young helper around the table to pick the little white flowers off the stalks, trying to remove as many of the tiny stalks as possible. It is a boring job for us grown-ups, but children like doing it and small hands are more capable.

Makes about 12 buns

100g unsalted butter
200g polenta flour
125g Italian 00 flour
1½ tsp baking powder
pinch of salt
125g caster sugar
1 organic egg, beaten
2 tbsp full-fat milk
6 tbsp elderflowers, stalks
    removed
pouring cream, to serve

Preheat the oven to 180°C/gas mark 4.

Melt the butter slowly in a saucepan. Meanwhile mix together all the dry ingredients in a bowl, then add the beaten egg, milk and the melted butter. The mixture should have a dropping consistency. Stir well and then shower with the flowers and gently mix them in.

Line a 12-hole jam tart tin with paper cases. Dollop equal amounts of the mixture into each case – another enjoyable job for small hands. Bake for about 20 minutes, until a cocktail stick comes out dry from the middle of the buns. Let them cool on a wire rack and then place each bun in the middle of a bowl and pour good thick cream all around it.

Ten-minute cake

When I saw this title in one of the Italian cookery books on my shelves, *La Cucina d'Oro*, I thought this is just the cake for me. A quick sponge that Coco and the other grandchildren can ice, decorate, fill or simply eat as it is. Perfect. So it became my standard recipe for a sponge cake. Sometimes we use the mixture to fill small cake cases, other times I use a ring mould and the cake looks stunning when it is served, set on a round dish with its hole filled with glistening raspberries, and with a jug of eggy custard to drown it in.

You will need an electric mixer with a flat beater attachment to make this speedy sponge cake.

Serves 6

100g Italian 00 flour
1½ tsp baking powder
pinch of sea salt
100g unsalted butter,
    just melted
100g golden caster sugar
2 organic eggs, at room
    temperature
grated rind of 1 organic lemon
    (or 3 drops pure vanilla
    extract)
melted butter and dried
    breadcrumbs (see p.12),
    for the tin

Preheat the oven to 180°C/gas mark 4.

Butter an 18cm springform cake tin, line it with parchment paper and then butter the paper. If you are using a ring mould, which is impossible to line with paper, you must butter it very generously, taking great care to cover every little bit, and then sprinkle some dried breadcrumbs all over the buttered surface.

Sieve the flour, baking powder and salt, letting them fall into a bowl from a height so that the mixture gets light and airy. Add all the other ingredients and then beat them all together with an electric mixer for 1 minute. The mixture will become pale in colour and fluffy, forming soft peaks. Spoon the mixture into the prepared tin, bang the tin on the work surface to settle the mixture and put it in the oven. Bake for 20–30 minutes until a cocktail stick pushed in the middle of the cake comes out dry. Remove the cake from the tin and let it cool on a wire rack. The cake is now ready for Coco to decorate or to make a trifle with, or to eat as it is … or you can wrap it in foil for dealing with later.

Coco's zuppa inglese

Zuppa inglese is the Italian answer to the English trifle. We make 2 variations, one with coffee, and the other with chocolate. Coco loves to put a little Cointreau in her *zuppa inglese*, because of its orangey flavour, but should your children object to the taste of alcohol, leave it out and add, instead, some grated orange peel.

Zuppa inglese with coffee

Serves 6–8
Ten-minute cake (see p.161)
150ml espresso coffee
4 tbsp Cointreau

For the custard:
450ml full-fat milk
yolks of 3 organic eggs
120g icing sugar, sifted
3 tbsp Italian 00 flour
½ tsp pure vanilla extract

For the decoration:
grated chocolate or
    chocolate balls
whipped cream

To make the custard, first heat the milk to just under boiling point. Whisk the egg yolks and the icing sugar together in a bowl until light and fluffy. Gradually add the flour while beating the whole time with a wooden spoon and then slowly pour in the hot milk together with the vanilla extract while you continue beating hard. Strain the mixture into a saucepan that has a very thick bottom and set the pan on a low heat. Cook while you go on beating constantly until the custard has thickened and a few bubbles break on the surface. Remove the pan from the heat and set aside. Coco always loves to make custard – it's one of her firm favourites.

Thickly cut the Ten-minute cake into slices about 4–5cm thick. Then mix together the espresso coffee and the Cointreau.

Get a nice glass bowl and spread 3–4 tablespoons of the custard over the bottom and then cover with a layer of cake slices. Dip a pastry brush into the coffee mixture and soak the cake with it. Cover with a thick layer of custard, and then with about a quarter of the cake slices. Now brush with the coffee mixture again, then add a layer of custard, cake and so on, finishing with a layer of cake soaked with coffee.

Cover the bowl with clingfilm and chill for at least 4 hours. Before you bring it to the table, ask your Coco to decorate it. My Coco likes to sprinkle it with grated chocolate or little chocolate balls, and then to put blobs of whipped cream here and there.

Zuppa inglese with chocolate

Serves 6–8

Instead of the coffee and Cointreau you will need 2 tablespoons rum and 4 tablespoons full-fat milk mixed together, plus 60g bitter chocolate.

Melt the chocolate in a bain-marie (i.e. in a heatproof bowl above a pan of simmering water). Make the custard as directed in the previous recipe. Pour half the custard into a bowl and mix in the melted chocolate. Now build up the pud, alternating layers of plain custard, cake soaked in the rum mixture, chocolate custard and then cake again until you have used all the ingredients, finishing, as in the previous recipe, with a layer of cake. Spread with a thin layer of whipped cream and decorate this *zuppa* with some chopped toasted almonds – about 30g.

Chocolate sauce

This is a very easy chocolate sauce, suitable for serving with most cakes and puddings. It is one of Coco's favourite sauces, possibly because of the 'licky licky' at the end.

200g dark chocolate
    (min. 70% cocoa solids)
150ml double cream
85g caster sugar

Break the chocolate up into small bits and put them in a small, heavy-based saucepan. Add 4 tablespoons of the cream and put the pan on the heat. Gently heat it until the chocolate has melted, stirring the whole time, and then add the sugar and the rest of the cream. Mix well and cook for a further minute. This is the perfect accompaniment to the Ten-minute cake on p.161.

Smoothie

The other day Coco brought me a cup full of a brown frothy liquid. Very suspiciously, I asked, 'What is it?' 'It is my smoothie for you,' she said. I am afraid I don't like smoothies, but this is a book for children and my preferences do not come into it. So here, in her own words, is the recipe for the smoothie Coco made.

Makes 4 small cups
1 mango
1 banana
4 tbsp natural yoghurt
2 tbsp caster sugar
2 tbsp runny honey
100ml full-fat milk

Peel the mango and cut it into small pieces. Do the same with the banana and then put them into the blender and whiz for 30 seconds. Add all the other ingredients and whiz again until smooth. Divide the mixture into 4 cups and drink it with a straw. ['A straw is essential,' Coco emphasised.]

Francesca's mousse

Francesca is a good friend of mine who used to make this chocolate mousse with her daughter. Coco and I made it a few times when I was teaching her how to separate eggs – not an easy job for a child. And then one day she proudly brought me a petit pot full of a brown mixture and said, 'Here you are, Nonna, Francesca's mousse.' And it was perfect.

Makes 4 small pots
3 eggs, separated
3 tbsp caster sugar
100g dark chocolate
   (min. 70% cocoa solids)
candied violets, to decorate
   (optional)

Whisk the egg whites until they form soft peaks and then, in a separate bowl, beat the yolks with the sugar until pale. (If you do the whites first, you can use the same whisk and save on washing-up, but *not* the other way round.) Break the chocolate into little pieces, put it in a suitable bowl and melt it in the microwave, which is the easiest way for a child, or in a bain-marie (i.e. in a heat proof bowl above a pan of simmering water). Mix the melted chocolate into the egg yolk and sugar mixture, and then fold in the egg white, trying to retain as much air as you can while you do it. Spoon the mousse into 4 small pots or ramekins. When I have some candied violets in the cupboard, Coco loves to place one in the middle of each pot, but, if I don't have them, she sticks an almond in the middle or spoons a blob of whipped cream over the top.

Fruit salad

All the children in my life have always loved fruit salad, and have learnt early on how to make a good one, which is not as easy as it sounds. First of all, they have learnt which fruits are essential, and which are not and so can be varied according to the season. I have also taught them to cut the fruit into smallish cubes, about 1–1.5cm, so that the juices can easily be absorbed. They know that all the fruit should be ripe but not overripe, just in perfect condition, and the salad must be prepared some time in advance for the flavours to develop and combine with each other.

Children might not like individual fruits, but they usually like fruit salad, and they also like preparing it.

Serves 6–8
2 dessert apples
2 pears
2 bananas
200g seedless red grapes
750g assorted seasonal fruit,
    such as peaches or
    nectarines, apricots,
    cherries, plums, kiwis
50g caster sugar
juice of 2 oranges
juice of 1 lemon

If the skin of the apples and pears is too tough, peel them. Otherwise, simply wash and dry them. Cut both fruits into small cubes and put them in a large bowl. Peel the bananas, slice them and add to the bowl. Wash the grapes and add to the bowl. All the other fruit should be washed (I don't peel peaches, but you might like to), dried and cut into similar small cubes, except for the cherries, which go in whole, as I never bother to take the stones out, except when there are very young children around the table. I think children should learn how to deal with fruit stones just as they should learn how to deal with fish bones. Cut the fruit on a plate so that all the juices can be collected and added to the bowl.

Sprinkle with the sugar and pour the juices from the oranges and lemon over the fruit. Mix thoroughly but gently, using 2 forks. Let your Coco taste and add more sugar if the mixture is too sharp. Cover the bowl with clingfilm and refrigerate for at least 2 hours.

Oria's brownies

Oria is my granddaughter Kate's best friend. A few months ago, the two girls came to my house carrying an offering on a plate: 2 dark, sticky-looking squares. 'These brownies are for you, Nonna; we made them with Coco and Basil' (Oria's brother). I am not particularly keen on brownies, nor am I a chocolate lover. But I took a suspicious bite and was overwhelmed by the incredibly delicious flavour that burst into my mouth. When I got my breath back I shouted, 'Wow, I want the recipe for the book!' And here it is.

These brownies are very rich and gooey and extremely moreish. They are best served straight out of the fridge.

Serves 8
125g unsalted butter
50g best-quality unsweetened
    cocoa powder
397g tin sweetened condensed
    milk
125ml full-fat milk
130g firmly packed brown sugar
2 tsp pure vanilla extract
100g plain flour
2 organic eggs, lightly beaten
200g dark chocolate
    (min. 70% cocoa solids)

Preheat the oven to 180°C/gas mark 4. Line a square cake tin with a ready-made liner or parchment paper.

Combine the butter, cocoa powder, condensed milk and milk in a heavy-based pan and put it on a low heat. Cook until the butter is completely melted, stirring constantly and taking care that the mixture does not stick to the bottom of the pan, as it can easily do. Add the sugar, vanilla extract and flour and mix thoroughly. After that, incorporate the eggs.

Break the chocolate into small pieces and add to the mixture. (Coco & Co. love to smash the wrapped bar with a mallet.) Stir the mixture until the chocolate has dissolved, and that's it. The mixture is ready to be poured into the prepared tin and baked. Bake for about 25 minutes until just firm to the touch and then let it cool in the tin.

When the cake is cold, place the tin in the fridge to chill. Before you want to serve the brownies, unmould the cake and cut it into 3cm squares. If you wish, you can let your Coco dust them with cocoa powder, but I find them chocolatey enough. Keep any leftover brownies in the fridge, although I doubt there will be any.

4
The Budding Chef

Now that she is 12, Coco has become quite sure of herself in the kitchen and enjoys doing her own cooking, far more, in fact, than she does cooking with me, as I tend to interfere and tell her how to do things my way. She can take decisions, and envisage, to some extent, the final result. She can also, at long last, actually *cook* – and by that I mean putting pots and pans on the heat or in the oven which she has previously turned on to the right temperature.

Whether she will become a fully-fledged chef is immaterial. What she will always be is a good cook who, I hope, will one day teach her own children the importance and the pleasure of good food in a family.

Pinzimonio *Raw vegetable dip*

When Julia, Coco's mother, was a child we spent all our summer holidays in our house in Chianti. The vegetables were, as they still are, superb and the best thing we could do with them was to eat them straight up, like that, with olive oil, of course, and certainly never naked. Rome has made the dish its own and called it *pinzimonio*.

Julia loved to make and eat *pinzimonio*, as indeed now Coco does when we are at their house in Le Marche. But you don't have to go to Chianti or Le Marche to make a good *pinzimonio*; you can make it anywhere, as long as you make it at the right time of year with local vegetables when they are in season.

Pinzimonio is the sort of dish any child who can safely handle a knife will enjoy making because they can choose their favourite veg and to a certain extent make the dressing that they fancy. Each eater has their own little bowl of dressing (traditionally only olive oil and salt), while the raw vegetables are piled up on a dish in the middle of the table in a most convivial way.

What follows is Coco's choice of vegetables and her personal dressing, which has the addition of a little balsamic vinegar. It works well, especially when you make *pinzimonio* in Britain, where the veg are less flavoursome than in Italy – the kick of the vinegar helps.

These are the vegetables we use: carrots, celery, fennel, tomatoes, cucumber, peppers, small courgettes, radishes, spring onions. You can add cauliflower, but I draw the line at raw asparagus, which I find inedible, however fashionable it might be in Britain. Coco's touch is to add avocado to the display.

I am not going to spell out the quantities; you prepare as many vegetables as you think you need. Just remember that it is always better to err on the side of generosity than meanness. You can always make a vegetable soup with the leftovers.

Wash and peel the carrots. If small, leave them as they are, otherwise, cut them lengthwise in half or even quarters. Remove the outside strings from the stalks of the celery, wash and cut into lengths of about 8cm. Wash and cut the cucumber to the same size, then cut each length into 4 sections. Do the same with the courgettes. Trim the fennel top and bottom, discard the blemished outer leaves and then cut the bulb lengthwise into 4 or 8 segments, depending on how large it is. Wash it well. Wash the peppers, cut in half, discard the core, seeds and ribs and cut lengthwise into strips of about 3cm. Wash the radishes and leave them as they are with the green top for decoration and ease of handling. Pull off and discard the outer leaves of the spring onion, cut off the roots and about 2cm off the top. If you have also chosen cauliflower, cut the head in half, then cut the florets off the stalk and wash them.

When all the vegetables are ready, let your Coco pile them up or make a pattern on a large platter and set the platter in the middle of the table.

For the dressing you need to fill each small bowl – I use 100ml ramekins – with the best extra-virgin olive oil (a peppery Tuscan oil is ideal) and then mix in a little sea salt. Coco mixes in about ½ teaspoon balsamic vinegar, while I like the same amount of lemon juice and a grinding of pepper. Johnny adds crushed chilli – he adds crushed chilli to everything. Hand around lots of kitchen paper; it will be needed.

Garlic soup

One wet afternoon Coco brought me a bowl full of beige liquid with a few green speckles floating in it. 'Not very attractive,' I thought, but then I put my finger in the liquid, licked it and said, 'Wow!'

'It's a garlic soup which I made with Tiger. I read the recipe in one of your magazines, Nonna, and I thought it was good. But as you always say, I changed it a bit. I put soured cream in instead of double cream, because that was the cream which I found in the fridge, and just a little nutmeg, because I love nutmeg.'

'Good,' I said, since I always encourage her to add her signature to whatever she cooks. And, because she was cooking for 6, she rightly increased the quantities. The magazine was *Sainsbury's magazine*, which Coco steals from my house even before I can set eyes on it. She swears it is the best of all cookery magazines.

Serves 6

3 large onions, chopped
1 garlic bulb
2 bay leaves
2 sprigs thyme
50g unsalted butter
3 tbsp olive oil
3 large potatoes
3 tsp Marigold Swiss vegetable
    bouillon powder
6 tbsp soured cream
pinch or 2 of grated nutmeg
small bunch of chives
sea salt, to taste

And here is how she wrote down the method:

I first sliced the onions and chopped them with the mezzaluna. Then I peeled the garlic cloves, all of them, one by one, and chopped them too with the mezzaluna. Then I put the onion, bay leaves, thyme, butter, oil and a little salt in the soup pot and cooked it very slowly until the onion was soft. I stirred quite a lot. After that I threw in the garlic and covered the pot with the lid and let it sweat for 10 minutes.

While the soup was sweating, I peeled the potatoes and cut them into small cubes, very small actually, about 1cm, and added them to the pot. And then I let the soup sweat for another 5 minutes.

After that, I boiled 1.5 litres water in the kettle. I put the Marigold powder in a cup and added a little water and mixed it, and then I spooned it into the pot. And then I added the rest of the boiling water, while Tiger was mixing with a long wooden spoon. And I let the soup cook for half an hour.

After that, I picked up the bay leaves and threw them away and I put the 'juje' into it and 'jujed' it.

[I asked what on earth the 'juje' was. And she told me that this is what she calls the stick blender, because of the noise it makes while it works.] When the soup was all 'jujed' I mixed in the cream and the grated nutmeg. After Mummy put the soup in the bowls, I cut a little chive in the middle of each bowl. We ate it, dipping in some slices of warm baguette.

Spaghetti alla puttanesca

Spaghetti with tomatoes, anchovies and olives

This is one of the dishes we cook when we do not know what else to have; it is easy, quick and delicious, and also handy, because all the necessary ingredients are always around. Unless I have very good fresh tomatoes, I prefer to use a good brand of tinned chopped tomatoes. And Coco does the same now that she cooks *puttanesca* by herself. We have compared the two and decided that the *puttanesca* with tinned tomatoes is better. Often, when I make *spaghetti alla puttanesca* I add an extra 100g of pasta so that there is some left over for Coco to take home and make a small pasta frittata all for herself the next day, which she loves.

Serves 4

500g ripe tomatoes, skinned, seeded and chopped, or 400g tin chopped tomatoes

5 tbsp extra-virgin olive oil

350g spaghetti

1 small fresh chilli, seeded and finely chopped (or more, depending on strength and taste)

4 salted anchovies, cleaned and chopped, or 8 anchovy fillets, drained and chopped

2 garlic cloves, chopped

2 tbsp capers, rinsed and dried

100g black olives, stoned

2 tbsp chopped flat-leaf parsley, to garnish

sea salt, to taste

If you are using fresh tomatoes, fry them in a saucepan in ½ tablespoon of the oil for 5 minutes. If you are using tinned tomatoes, fry them for 3 minutes, turning them over frequently.

Drop the pasta into a pan of fast-boiling, salted water and cook until al dente. Meanwhile, put a frying pan on the heat, large enough to hold the pasta later, add the remaining oil, the chilli, anchovies and garlic and fry over a low heat for 2 minutes, mashing the anchovies to a paste with a fork or a wooden spoon. Spoon in the tomatoes and, after 2 minutes, add the capers and olives. Time for Coco to taste and check the seasoning. It might need a little salt. Mix well and, as soon as the pasta is done, drain it and throw it in the *puttanesca* pan. Stir-fry for 2–3 minutes, shower with the parsley, mix and serve.

Bucatini all'Amatriciana

Bucatini with spicy tomato and pancetta sauce

This is, at the moment, Coco's favourite pasta sauce. She has always liked it, even when she was very young and I used to make it a little less hot. You can do the same, adapting it slightly to please your Coco. This is my original recipe revisited by Coco (less wine, more onion), who now makes the sauce totally by herself and serves it with penne, simply because penne are her favourite pasta shape. But *bucatini* (spaghetti-like tubes) are the traditional shape for *Amatriciana* and usually all children love them because they are fun to suck up.

Serves 4–5

1 tbsp olive oil
350g unsmoked pancetta cubes
1 onion, very finely chopped
1 garlic clove, finely chopped
1 dried chilli, seeded and
    finely chopped
100ml red wine
450g tin chopped tomatoes
400g *bucatini*
6 tbsp grated mature pecorino
sea salt and freshly ground
    black pepper, to taste
freshly grated Parmigiano-
    Reggiano, to serve

Heat the oil in a frying pan large enough to contain the cooked pasta later and, when hot, throw in the pancetta and fry until crisp. Remove it to a plate with a fish slice. Now add the onion to the pan, season with a pinch of salt and sauté for 7–8 minutes, until soft. Add the garlic and chilli and cook for a further minute, stirring frequently. Splash with the wine and let it bubble away to reduce by half. Pour in the chopped tomatoes and cook on a moderate heat for about 20–25 minutes. Taste – your Coco's job – and add more salt if necessary and black pepper if you want, although the sauce is already quite hot due to the chilli.

Cook the *bucatini* in plenty of salted water as usual. Drain thoroughly, giving the colander a few sharp shakes so that the water trapped in the holes of the *bucatini* comes out. Slide the pasta into the frying pan, shower with the pecorino and stir-fry for about 2 minutes, turning the *bucatini* over and over with 2 forks. Serve straight from the pan, with Parmesan handed round.

Eggs in the nest

This is really *tagliatelle alla carbonara* presented in a way that is more fun to make and to see. And Coco loves to separate eggs, now that she has learned how to do it, after many disasters. I use tagliatelle instead of the usual *bucatini* or spaghetti for this sauce, because tagliatelle are easier to shape into a 'nest'. I don't always make the tagliatelle; more often I buy a very good Italian brand of dried egg tagliatelle. You can use unsmoked or smoked pancetta, whatever your children prefer.

Serves 4

75g unsalted butter
2 tbsp olive oil
12 sage leaves, coarsely chopped
1 garlic clove, squashed
125g pancetta cubes
200g dried egg tagliatelle
6 tbsp freshly grated
    Parmigiano-Reggiano,
    plus more for serving
4 organic egg yolks
sea salt and freshly ground
    black pepper, to taste

Preheat the oven to 180°C/gas mark 4.

First heat the butter and the oil in a frying pan with the sage and the garlic. When the fat begins to sizzle, retrieve the garlic and discard it (you might like to leave it in, in which case, chop it or crush it). Pour the hot fat into a cup and keep it warm in a bowl full of hot water.

Now put the pancetta into the same frying pan and sauté it until crisp, while you cook the tagliatelle in plenty of boiling salted water. When the pasta is al dente, set aside a mugful of the pasta water before you drain it. Never overdrain tagliatelle or any egg pasta. Put the pasta back into the saucepan and pour over it the reserved hot butter and oil mixture, toss very well and then mix in the cheese and black pepper to taste, and add some of the pasta water if it seems too dry.

Now take a baking tray and smear it lightly with oil. With a fork, lift out a forkful or two of tagliatelle and plonk it on the tray, shaping it like a nest, with a hollow in the middle. Spoon a few bits of pancetta into the hollow, drop a yolk into it, and repeat with the remaining tagliatelle until you have 4 nests. Place the baking tray in the oven for 8–10 minutes. The yolks should still be soft all through.

Transfer the nests to heated plates and serve with more Parmesan on the side.

Chicken wings
in a garlicky green crust

This is a dish you can vary according to your Coco's preferences, and to what you have in the cupboard. It is an undemanding dish that is always a children's favourite, mostly because they can eat it with their hands.

Years ago Germaine Greer gave a lecture at the Guild of Food Writers on the subject of Sex and Food. She started the talk with this arresting sentence: 'Don't think I am here to talk about f...ing and eating. I am here to tell you the different approach boys and girls have to food.' A good opening, and the talk was indeed fascinating in pointing out how girls react much more instinctively and directly to what they put in their mouths. Boys, faced with a chicken wing on their plate, for instance, would look at it, turn it over with a fork and try to cut it up with the knife, a girl would usually pick it up in her hands and gnaw it. This is the sort of dish that makes a girl happy and a boy too, actually, after the first moments of bewilderment.

This is my basic crust but you might prefer a different type of crust: a tablespoon of olive paste, for instance, instead of the capers; no chilli and garlic but some finely chopped spring onion; 1 or 2 chopped anchovy fillets or some coriander instead of a little parsley. All perfect.

Serves 4

12 organic chicken wings
large bunch flat-leaf parsley
small handful of fresh
    marjoram (optional)
2 garlic cloves
grated rind of 1 organic lemon
pinch or 2 of dried crushed chilli
1 tbsp capers, rinsed and
    drained
2 tbsp dried white breadcrumbs
    (see p.12)
1 tsp sea salt
5 tbsp extra-virgin olive oil

Pluck the chicken wings clean of any quills, wash and dry them carefully. Open them up and flatten them down with your fist.

To prepare the crust, chop together the parsley, marjoram and garlic and put in a bowl. Mix in the lemon rind, chilli, capers, breadcrumbs and salt. Pour in 3 tablespoons of the oil and stir well. Give a spoon to your Coco to check the seasoning. Now pat this mixture into the chicken wings so that they are well covered with it – the perfect job for small hands. Pat hard; most of the crust must stick. Brush a baking tray with a little of the remaining oil and put the chicken on it. Scoop all the bits of crust left loose over the chicken and douse with the remaining olive oil. Place the tray in the fridge or, better, in the larder, if you still have one of those almost extinct cubbyholes, for about 2 hours.

Preheat the oven to 220°C/gas mark 7.

Put the tray in the oven, turn the heat down to 200°C/gas mark 6 and cook for 15–20 minutes. Let the dish cool a little before you bring it to the table. You don't want little hands to get burnt in the enthusiasm of the assault. Coco likes these chicken wings with the Roasted vegetables on p.186.

Roasted vegetables

Coco likes to have these vegetables alongside the Chicken wings (p.184), and preparing them is nearly as much fun as eating them. This is my spring and summer roasted vegetable dish, while in the autumn we use seasonal vegetables like butternut squash, leeks, potatoes and sweet potatoes.

I roast the vegetables in the oven first and then remove them before I turn the oven up for the chicken wings. While the chicken is cooking I cover the veg with a piece of foil and leave them to cool down to the ideal temperature. But if you prefer them hotter, put the dish back in the oven for the last 5 minutes while the chicken wings finish cooking.

Serves 4

1 red pepper
1 yellow pepper
1 green pepper
1 aubergine, about 300g
200g medium-sized courgettes
300g red onions, very finely
    sliced
2 tbsp tomato passata
5 tbsp extra-virgin olive oil
1 tbsp chopped fresh mint
½ tbsp dried oregano
2 tbsp chopped flat-leaf parsley
2 garlic cloves, finely sliced
sea salt and freshly ground
    black pepper, to taste

Preheat the oven to 180°C/gas mark 4.

First prepare the vegetables. Wash and dry the peppers, cut into quarters and remove the seeds, cores and ribs. Wash and dry the aubergine, cut it in half and then cut each half into thickish slices, about 5mm. Do the same with the courgettes. See that the slices are more or less all of the same thickness.

Oil a rectangular oven tray, spread the onion all over the bottom and then drop blobs of passata here and there. Drizzle with 1 tablespoon of the oil and season lightly with salt and pepper. The tray is now ready for Coco to put the vegetables in the way she likes, which varies according to her mood. They look attractive laid in alternative strips over the oniony bottom. Sprinkle with the herbs and the garlic and drizzle with the remaining oil. Roast until the vegetables are soft, which should take about 1½ hours.

Johnny's chicken

This recipe is really 'Cooking with Johnny' not 'Cooking with Coco'. My 14-year-old grandson is a passionate eater more than a passionate cook. But for this reason he is extremely interested in food and knows what he likes, an attitude with which I very much sympathise. A few years ago – he must have been about 11 at the time – he kept pestering me to make a chicken like the one he'd had at a friend's house. I realised then that it was time he cooked something on his own. The dish seemed easy enough and its preparation seemed very safe to me. So I told him, 'If you tell me what to buy, you can make it for me at the weekend.' He gave me the list, a very short list, just as I like; in fact, I already had everything in the house apart from the chicken breasts. And the dish he produced was so good that, now I am alone, I make it quite often for myself: quick, easy and full of flavour.

Serves 2

4 tbsp olive oil, plus more
    for serving
2 onions, very finely sliced
2 tsp cumin seeds
200g tin chopped tomatoes
½ tsp dried crushed chilli
2 tsp paprika
250g chicken breasts, skinned
boiling water, from a kettle
sea salt and freshly ground
    black pepper, to taste

Heat the oil in a heavy-based sauté pan and, when hot, throw in the onion and cook for 10 minutes, turning the onion over frequently. 'Now, Nonna,' explained Johnny, 'what I did was to push the onion around the side of the pan and spoon the cumin seeds in the middle, so that they could roast lightly. I did it like that because I didn't want to dirty another pan.' After a couple of minutes, add the tomatoes and a little salt and cook for 2 or 3 minutes over a moderate heat. Turn the heat right down and cook very slowly for about 30 minutes. Halfway through the cooking, season with the chilli, paprika and some black pepper. Keep an eye on it and if it gets too dry, add 2–3 tablespoons boiling water.

While the sauce is cooking, wash and dry the chicken breast and cut it into slices about 5mm thick. When the sauce looks dense, turn the heat up a little and throw in the chicken slices. Cook for 3 minutes, add 3 or 4 tablespoons boiling water and then turn the heat down and cook for a few more minutes; 5 or 6 minutes should be all that's needed, but it depends on how thick the slices are and how high the heat is. To see if the chicken is cooked, cut a thickish slice in half and ask your Coco – or your Johnny – to have a look so that she (or he) can learn when a piece of chicken is cooked: when the flesh is no longer pink. Serve it on a bed of basmati rice, dressed with 1 tablespoon olive oil, or on a bed of couscous, also anointed with a little oil.

Kebabs

Coco has been an avid kebab-maker and eater since an early age. She liked to be able to choose some of the ingredients and to show her dexterity in threading them on to the skewers. Now she makes kebabs all by herself; she simply gives me the list for the shopping. I am sure all children would enjoy making and eating them.

Kebabs have the added advantage for a child that, once they are prepared, it takes only a few minutes before the end product is ready to eat.

Here are 3 basic recipes for three different types of kebabs. But you can diversify and change according to your Coco's taste or what you have in the fridge. Experimenting is half the fun of cooking.

Monkfish kebabs

This dish is really 'Teaching Nonna how to cook', since Coco told me what to do with the monkfish I bought. I usually cook fish in my Italian way, which consists simply of roasting, grilling or steaming it, without the addition of any other ingredients, olive oil apart, so that the flavour of the fish isn't marred, or at least altered by unnecessary additions. But I have to admit that this recipe is very good and, oddly enough, the marinating of the fish in the soy sauce seems to enhance the flavour of the monkfish and not distract from it.

Monkfish is ideal to give to children who are not keen on eating fish, as I have found out with my granddaughter Nell, who is a reluctant fish-eater. Monkfish doesn't taste particularly fishy, added to which it has solid meat and no bones – all points in its favour.

Serves 4
400g monkfish
10g root ginger
1 garlic clove
2½ tbsp dark soy sauce
2 red peppers
6 cherry tomatoes
1 red onion, thickly sliced
freshly ground black pepper,
    to taste

Cut the monkfish into cubes of about 3cm and put them in a bowl. Peel the ginger, chop it together with the garlic and add to the bowl. Pour over them the soy sauce, then season with pepper (no salt is needed because of the soy) and mix well so that all the fish pieces are well coated. Cover the bowl with clingfilm and place it in the fridge for at least 2 hours (it doesn't matter if you leave it a little longer; up to 3 hours is alright).

Wash and dry the peppers and tomatoes. Remove and discard the seeds, cores and ribs of the peppers and cut the flesh into squares. Cut the tomatoes in half. Turn on the grill to the highest setting and start preparing the kebabs with the help of your Coco.

Thread a piece of pepper on to a skewer, followed by a piece of fish, then a slice of onion, another chunk of fish, and then half a tomato, and continue like that, alternating the fish with the veg of your choice and finishing with a piece of vegetable. I thread each skewer with 3 chunks of monkfish in between different vegetable pieces.

After that, put the kebabs into an oiled grill pan or on an oiled baking tray and place the pan under the grill, not too close to the heat. Cook for 5 minutes, turning the kebabs over halfway through the cooking. Use oven gloves; the metal skewers are hot. When the kebabs are ready, put them on a dish in the middle of the table and let them cool a little before you call your Coco to eat. Or, if you are worried about little hands getting burnt, slide the pieces off the skewers directly onto the plates.

Chicken kebabs

I make these kebabs with chicken thighs not breasts, because I find that the meat of the breast is too dry for grilling. You could also add chunks of courgette, which would go well with the other ingredients.

Serves 4

350g skinless and boneless
    chicken thighs
3 tbsp olive oil
2 garlic cloves, chopped
bunch of flat-leaf parsley,
    chopped
150g button mushrooms,
    wiped with a damp cloth
    and dried
1 tbsp balsamic vinegar
1 red onion
150g unsmoked pancetta cubes
sea salt and freshly ground
    black pepper, to taste

Cut the chicken into cubes of about 3cm and put them in a bowl. Heat the olive oil in a small frying pan and add the garlic and parsley. Fry for 1 minute, then add the mushrooms and fry for 5 more minutes, turning them over and over in the oil. Season with salt and pepper and then add to the chicken in the bowl, scraping down all the bits that are sticking to the pan. Add the balsamic vinegar to the bowl and mix well – small hands are the best tool. Cover the bowl and put it aside for 2 hours or so. Don't put the bowl in the fridge as you want to grill the chicken at room temperature.

Get your metal skewers ready and call your Coco. Cut the onion into thick slices. I start by threading a piece of onion, followed by a chunk of chicken, then a mushroom, then a pancetta cube and an onion piece, chicken etc., finishing always with the onion. Our kebabs usually have 2 pieces of chicken each plus the rest, but you can have 3 pieces – it would not make any difference. Place the kebabs in an oiled grill pan or on an oiled baking tray.

Heat the grill to the highest setting and then place the kebabs under the grill, not too close to the heat. Grill for 7–8 minutes and then turn the kebabs over and leave for a further 5 minutes. Don't forget to wear oven gloves when you turn them over or you will burn your hands on the metal skewers. At the end, the chicken should be deliciously browned at the edges. Unload the kebabs directly onto individual plates, or wait a few minutes and then let your Coco manage the unscrewing. Coco loves these with couscous, and so do I.

Pork kebabs

Sometimes we make these with chunks of sausage. The best sausages to use are the plain ones, without added flavouring, because you are going to add your own. Just make sure that the sausages have a high content of pure pork meat.

I prefer to use metal skewers because they conduct the heat far better, but if you use them too, you must remember that they will get very hot by the end of the cooking.

Serves 4

450g pork tenderloin
3 tbsp olive oil
2 tsp balsamic vinegar
grated rind and juice of
   1 organic lemon
a few sprigs fresh thyme
sprig of fresh rosemary
2 garlic cloves
1 chilli, seeded
3 yellow peppers
12 cherry tomatoes
1 large red onion
sea salt and freshly ground
   black pepper, to taste

Cut the pork into 2cm slices and, if the slices are large, cut each slice in half. Put them in a bowl and pour over them 2 tablespoons of the oil, the 2 teaspoons vinegar and the lemon rind. Scrape the leaves and needles off the thyme and the rosemary sprigs and chop them together with the garlic and the chilli. Add to the bowl and season with salt and pepper. Mix well so that every bit of meat is shining with oil and speckled with the herbs. Cover the bowl with clingfilm and set aside for about 2 hours. You don't need to put the bowl in the fridge unless the weather is very hot. All meat marinates far better at room temperature and also it should never be cooked straight from the fridge.

Wash and dry the peppers, cut them into quarters, then remove and discard the core, seeds and ribs. Now cut the peppers into 2–3cm pieces. Wash and dry the tomatoes and cut them in half. Thickly slice the onion. Put all the vegetable pieces into a bowl, pour the remaining 1 tablespoon oil over them and season with a little salt and pepper.

Now everything is ready for your Coco to start threading. I like to start with a veg and thread the pork in between 2 pieces of onion, which can flavour the meat and supply some moisture. So, here it goes: peppers, onion, pork, onion, tomato, onion, pork, onion and so on. Lay the kebabs in an oiled grill pan or on an oiled baking tray.

Heat the grill to the highest setting. Put the kebabs

under the grill but not too close to the heat. Grill for about 12–15 minutes, depending on how thick the pieces of pork are, and then, armed with an oven glove, slide the chunks off the skewers straight onto individual plates. Put the lemon juice in a small jug and pass the jug around. Coco and I like this final blessing.

Lamb with couscous

As Coco's latest passion is for Moroccan food, every now and then we have to cook one of the dishes chosen from her mother's Moroccan cookbook. I too love North African food, but I am no good at following recipes; I need to put my stamp on the dishes I am cooking. So this is my version of Moroccan lamb, which Coco and I created together. She was delighted with the result.

Serves 6

1kg shoulder of lamb,
    boned weight
4 tbsp olive oil
juice of 1 lemon
¼ tsp saffron
¼ tsp turmeric
1 tsp ground cinnamon
1 tsp mace
500g onions
100g almonds
400g tin chickpeas, drained
sea salt and freshly ground
    black pepper, to taste
1 tbsp chopped coriander,
    to garnish

For the couscous:
250g couscous
250ml boiling water,
    from a kettle
2 tbsp extra-virgin olive oil
1 tsp sea salt

Trim the lamb of fat and gristle, cut the meat into 2cm cubes and put it in a bowl.

Beat together with a fork 2 tablespoons of the oil and half the lemon juice. Season with salt and pepper and pour into the bowl with the lamb. Mix the meat around to coat all of it and leave for 2–3 hours. (Do not chill it.) Then put the meat and the marinade in a large earthenware cooking pot (one that has a lid) and add the spices and the remaining oil. Pour over enough water to come level with the lamb and then bring slowly to the boil. Put the lid on the pot slightly askew, to leave an opening for the steam to escape so that the cooking juices will become more concentrated. Cook for about 1 hour, turning over the meat occasionally.

Meanwhile prepare the couscous. Put it in a bowl and pour 250ml boiling water over it. Leave for about 20 minutes and then fluff it up with a fork to make it lighter and to separate the grains. Add the olive oil and the salt and fork through it again. Keep warm in a low oven while you finish the lamb.

Slice the onions and mix into the pot together with the almonds and the chickpeas. Cook for a further 30 minutes or so, adding a little boiling water if the meat looks too dry. Taste and, with your Coco's help, check the lemon juice, spices and seasoning. Ladle it over the couscous and serve garnished with the coriander.

Pork fillet in spicy sauce

This dish is a 'Cooking with Coco and Dad' creation. One day, Coco decided she wanted to prepare a meal for lunch by herself, or nearly so. The fridge was not very full that day; there were only some pork fillets, just enough to make something.

Coco told her father what she had in mind. A dish with the flavour of a barbecue but with a little more 'grrr'. The grrr flavour was acidity, her father realised. So this sauce was born. Coco brought me a plateful of the dish to taste and comment on and I felt it was good enough to deserve a place in this book.

Serves 4

500g pork fillet
1 tbsp olive oil, plus 2 tbsp
    for frying
2 tbsp light soy sauce
1 tbsp balsamic vinegar
½ tsp sea salt
1 tbsp muscovado sugar
2 garlic cloves, crushed
juice of 1 organic lemon
grated rind of ½ organic lemon
a very few drops Tabasco sauce
freshly ground black pepper,
    to taste

Cut the fillet into 5mm-thick slices and put aside while you prepare the marinade. Gradually combine the 1 tablespoon oil and all the other ingredients in a bowl, beating well with a fork after each addition. When everything is thoroughly mixed, taste and check the lemon juice and salt, which are both essential to bring out the flavour of all the other ingredients. Add the meat and turn it until you can see that all the slices are well covered by the sauce. An agreeably messy job. Cover the bowl with clingfilm or a plate and leave for about 1 hour. Do not put the bowl in the fridge, because meat should always be cooked at room temperature, not chilled.

No more than 10 minutes before you want to eat, heat the remaining 2 tablespoons oil in a frying pan. When the oil is hot, lift the meat out of the marinade with a slotted spoon and add to the pan. Fry over a high heat until it is golden brown on both sides and then add the marinade. Mix well, allow it to cook for another 2 or 3 minutes and that's it: the dish is ready to bring to the table.

It is good with couscous or with boiled basmati rice.

Duck breasts in balsamic vinegar

My grandson Johnny loves good food (of which, he says, he doesn't get enough at boarding school), and his favourite meat is duck. When he comes home for the holidays, Coco and I like to prepare this dish for his first treat. It is delicious, quick and easy; the perfect recipe.

Serves 2–3
2 duck breasts, about 350g
3 spring onions, white part only
1 tbsp olive oil
3 tbsp balsamic vinegar
4–6 tbsp boiling water,
    from a kettle
sea salt and freshly ground
    black pepper, to taste

Score the skin of the duck breasts with the point of a sharp knife, deep enough to just penetrate the flesh underneath. Season with salt and pepper. Cut the spring onions into small pieces.

Put the oil in a non-stick frying pan and, when hot, throw in the spring onions. Fry them for 5 minutes on a low heat until golden and then remove them with a fish slice and set aside while you cook the duck.

Turn the heat up and put the duck breasts into the pan, skin side down. Fry for 10 minutes, moving them around often so that they don't stick to the pan. Turn the breasts over and cook for 5 minutes more, then take them out and place them on a plate. Cut the breasts into slanting slices about 1cm thick. The meat should still be quite rare. However, in my experience, children are not keen on very rare meat, so for them I put the slices back in the pan to cook for a little longer.

Put the spring onions back into the pan and, when hot, spoon in the vinegar. Be careful because the vinegar will spit a lot, so keep your Coco at a distance. Cook, stirring the whole time, for 2 minutes while adding a little boiling water – about 4–6 tablespoons in all. Return the sliced duck and all the juices that have collected in the plate to the pan and finish cooking – we cook it for 1 minute, mixing it around, but you might like to leave it a little longer. Taste the juices to check the seasoning before you serve the dish.

This is a rich dish which needs only a few small boiled potatoes and some spinach with it.

Swiss chard torte

Last September Coco made this vegetable cake all on her own, after having made it with me once or twice previously. That month, Swiss chard was flourishing in her mother's vegetable garden and needed cutting every other day. This is Coco's recipe based on one of mine, which originally comes from one of the best Italian books I have on vegetable torte, pies and tarts.

Coco likes making this, firstly because she loves eating it and secondly because she enjoys the preparation of the chard. I have shown her how to cut the leaf from the stalk with a sharp strike down each side of the white stalk. (I keep the white stalk so that I can cook it later, covered with cheese sauce and baked.) You could use spinach here, but the flavour of the cake would be less delicate.

Serves 4–5

15g dried porcini mushrooms
50g good-quality white bread, crusts removed
150–200ml full-fat milk
300g floury potatoes
300g Swiss chard, green leaves only
120ml extra-virgin olive oil
2 garlic cloves, chopped
large bunch of flat-leaf parsley, stalks removed, chopped
4 organic eggs
80g Parmigiano-Reggiano, freshly grated
generous grating of nutmeg
2 tbsp chopped fresh marjoram or oregano
50g dried breadcrumbs (see p.12)
sea salt and freshly ground black pepper, to taste
12 cherry tomatoes, to serve

Soak the dried porcini in a cupful of hot water for 20 minutes or so. Cut the bread into pieces, put it in a bowl, then pour over enough milk to cover it and leave it to soak. Peel the potatoes, cut them into chunks and boil them in a large saucepan of salted water for 10 minutes. Roughly cut the Swiss chard, add to the same saucepan and cook until the potatoes are tender. Drain very thoroughly and, wearing rubber gloves, squeeze out all the water from the Swiss chard. Coarsely purée the whole thing with a stick blender – an ideal job for a child – because you don't want a smooth purée, but a rough one with bits in it. It is always easier to purée vegetables, especially potatoes, when they are hot.

Preheat the oven to 180°C/gas mark 4.

Drain, dry and chop the porcini. Squeeze all the milk out of the bread. Heat about three-quarters of the oil in a frying pan and, when it's hot, sauté the garlic, parsley, porcini, squeezed-out bread, potatoes and Swiss chard for 7 or 8 minutes, turning the mixture over frequently. Take the pan off the heat and let the mixture cool down a little. Mix in the eggs, one at a time, then the cheese, nutmeg, marjoram or oregano and the dried breadcrumbs. Season with salt and pepper, mix thoroughly, and then ask your Coco to taste it.

Brush a 20cm springform cake tin with some of the remaining oil, spoon the mixture into it and pour over all the remaining oil. Bake for 30–35 minutes. Let the torte cool down in the tin and then unmould it just before serving it. This is good served warm or cold with cherry tomatoes or a tomato salad.

Fried cauliflower

(and other vegetables)

I do not suggest that you should let your Coco do the deep-frying here, because that is one of the most difficult methods of cooking and it is also dangerous. But I bet she would love to prepare the vegetables to be fried and then watch you do the rest. Frying is very quick and the oil bubbling around the battered vegetables is fascinating to watch. And I would be very surprised if the fried vegetables didn't disappear into hungry mouths in no time at all.

Here is the recipe for fried cauliflower, but you can cook tomatoes, courgettes, or aubergines in the same way and they are all divine.

Serves 4
1 cauliflower
2–3 tbsp plain flour
1 egg, lightly beaten
sea salt, to taste
vegetable oil, for frying

Prepare the cauliflower by detaching the florets from the central stalk. (Keep the stalks for a vegetable soup.) See that all the florets are small and more or less the same size. Wash and dry them very well with kitchen paper. Then blanch them for 3–4 minutes in boiling salted water.

Spoon the flour into a freezer bag. Throw in the cauliflower florets, shake the bag and then empty it onto a board. Pick up the florets one by one, shake them lightly and then coat them in the beaten egg. This is the sort of little job children love to do, because of the attraction of watching the egg slithering along the vegetable and falling back into the bowl.

While your Coco is coating the florets, heat a wok or a frying pan with enough vegetable oil to come about 4cm up the sides of the pan. Now take over the cooking operation and let your Coco watch from a safe distance. When the oil is hot, but not smoking, pick up the coated florets one by one and slide them into the hot oil, gently but quickly so as to avoid drops of boiling oil landing on your hand. Do not crowd too many florets in the pan or the vegetables will not fry properly. While they are frying, I cover the pan with a mesh screen to contain the spattering. Fry the florets for 4–5 minutes and then lift them out with a slotted spoon and put them to drain in a dish lined with kitchen paper. Sprinkle them with salt and keep them warm in the oven until you have fried them all. Serve as soon as they are all done, just as they are – hot and crispy without any distracting sauces.

Roasted-vegetable calzone

Recently, Coco and her sister Nell came back from school declaring that they had eaten the best calzone ever. Calzone is a folded-over pizza, stuffed with local vegetables and traditional flavourings, which is made in most regions of Southern Italy. The calzone that my granddaughters enthused about was made by the English cook at their school, St Mary's in Shaftesbury. How things have changed!

Coco asked the cook for the recipe and we made it at home. I am delighted to say, the calzone of the Dorset school passed the tasting scrutiny of a real Italian cook – me. So here it is.

Serves 8

2–3 medium courgettes
2 red peppers
½ aubergine
6 cherry tomatoes
1 large red onion, thickly sliced
100ml extra-virgin olive oil
60g mozzarella, grated
2 garlic cloves, finely chopped
1 tbsp dried oregano
450g ciabatta bread dough mix
60g mature Cheddar, grated
sea salt and freshly ground
    black pepper, to taste

Preheat the oven to 180°C/gas mark 4.

Wash and dry the courgettes, peppers, aubergine and tomatoes. Cut the courgettes and aubergine into 3cm cubes. Remove and discard the cores, ribs and seeds from the peppers and cut the peppers into similar-sized pieces. Cut the tomatoes in half. Put all these vegetables, together with the sliced onion, in a roasting tray and pour over all the oil, but for 1 tablespoon. Add the mozzarella, garlic and oregano and season with salt and pepper. Mix thoroughly (little hands do a good job of this).

Put the tray in the oven and bake for 45 minutes or so. When all the vegetables are well roasted, remove from the oven and let them cool a little.

Make the bread dough, following the manufacturer's instructions, and then roll out the dough into an oval about 1.5–2cm thick. Transfer the rolled-out dough to an oiled baking tray and pile all the roasted vegetables over one half of the dough, leaving a clean border of about 2cm. Shower with the grated Cheddar and then, with your fingers, dampen the border with water. Now fold over the other half of the dough, pressing the edges together tightly so that no juice can escape. Our calzone looked more like a half-moon than a trouser leg, the meaning of the Italian word. Make 4 slits in the top of the calzone to allow the steam to escape. Brush all over with the remaining olive oil and bake for 40–45 minutes until the crust is crisp and golden. Serve hot, but not too hot.

Yummy cake

My granddaughter Kate decided on the name of this cake which Coco made from scratch, inspired by the recipe for Banana Bread she found in *How to be a Domestic Goddess* by Nigella Lawson. This book has become her Bible – forget Nonna's books.

   Her version of the cake came about quite naturally, so to speak. She decided to eliminate a few ingredients she does not like and to incorporate those she prefers. Otherwise Coco stuck to the original recipe. The result was indeed yummy, especially when the cake was still warm.

Serves 8–10

175g Italian 00 flour
2 tsp baking powder
½ tsp bicarbonate of soda
½ tsp salt
125g unsalted butter, melted
150g caster sugar
2 organic eggs
4 small ripe bananas, about
    300g weighed without
    the skin
60g pecan nuts,
    roughly chopped
1 tsp pure vanilla extract
50g dark chocolate
    (min. 70% cocoa solids)

Preheat the oven to 170°C/gas mark 3.

   Sieve the flour, baking powder and bicarbonate of soda into a bowl, stir in the salt and mix everything together (small hands do the trick very nicely).

   In another bowl, mix together the melted butter and sugar and then add the eggs, one at a time, beating well after each addition. Mash the bananas with a fork and add them to this butter mixture, together with the pecan nuts and the vanilla extract. Gradually add the flour mixture to this, mixing thoroughly with a metal spoon. When the mixture looks well blended, spoon it into a 20cm springform cake tin, which you have buttered and lined with parchment paper.

   Melt the chocolate in a bain-marie (i.e. in a heatproof bowl above a pan of simmering water) or in the microwave according to the manufacturer's instructions, and then pour it into the cake mixture. Give the mixture a stir or two so that the melted chocolate creates a marbled effect without combining completely. Place the tin in the oven and bake for 1 hour, until a cocktail stick inserted in the middle comes out clean. Leave the cake in the tin to cool for about half an hour and then unmould.

Double-chocolate-chip
biscuits

This is a recipe Coco taught me to make when she was 10. She made the biscuits all on her own while I was sitting down and watching, delighted to exchange roles at last. I was very impressed: they are delicious.

Makes about 30 biscuits
240g self-raising flour
60g best-quality unsweetened
    cocoa powder
240g unsalted butter, at room
    temperature
150g caster sugar
1 tsp vanilla essence
50g chocolate chips

Preheat the oven to 180°C/gas mark 4.

Sieve the flour and the cocoa powder. In a separate bowl, cream together the butter and the sugar very thoroughly and then gradually mix in the flour and cocoa, spoonful by spoonful. Add the vanilla and the chocolate chips. Mix thoroughly until the mixture looks smooth. You can do all this in a freestanding mixer.

Take dollops of the biscuit mixture the size of small walnuts, roll them into balls in the palms of your hands and place each ball on a lined baking tray, leaving a 4–5cm space between each ball, because the biscuits will spread during cooking. If you keep your hands moistened with warm water, you can roll a smoother ball. Lightly flatten each ball down with the wet prongs of a fork to give each biscuit a pretty top, like a grille. Place the tray in the oven and bake for 12–13 minutes.

Let the biscuits cool for some 10 minutes on the tray before transferring to a wire rack to cool completely.

Bananas in custard

I have been persuaded to include this recipe by my oldest granddaughter, Nell. This is her favourite pud, which she loves making because it is so easy. At first I thought it was far too simple to be written down, but then, when I published my recipe for Spaghetti with Marmite in my memoir, *Risotto with Nettles*, I realised how often we can ignore the simplest things. Everybody picked up on the recipe and Nigella Lawson was cross with me for not having given it to her earlier.

I made this pudding for my sons, Paul and Guy, when they were at school, using Bird's Eye Custard. I have never been a great pudding maker or eater, so I was quite happy to provide something the children enjoyed that was easy and quick. But Bird's Eye Custard tasted too synthetic for me, and soon enough I was making it with my own egg custard, so that I too could enjoy the pud. Since then it has remained in my repertoire. I resort to it quite often because I always have eggs and bananas in the house and rarely enough time to make something more complicated. We use the discarded egg whites to make meringues, which go very well with this.

Coco loves the pud sprinkled with cinnamon, but you can sprinkle it with poppy seeds or cardamom seeds, or you can flavour the custard with vanilla or lemon peel and leave the top unadorned. Chopped pistachio nuts are also a delicious and pretty topping. Coco likes to divide it all between individual bowls, as most children do. I always prefer to bring a generous single dish to the table, but this is a book to please children, so we decided to use the bowls, in which case each child can add their favourite topping. I use organic bananas because I find that, in this dish, they make a positive difference to the flavour.

Serves 6

yolks of 3 organic eggs
3 heaped tbsp caster sugar
300ml single cream
4 organic bananas

First make the custard, which is, actually, not as easy as it seems. Now that she is 12, Coco can make it on her own, because she has learned to be patient and she knows quite a lot about cooking.

Put the egg yolks in a saucepan and add the sugar. Beat hard with a wooden spoon for 2 or 3 minutes and then put the pan on a low heat and gradually add the cream. Slowly does it, while you continue beating. After some 5–8 minutes you will feel the custard getting slightly thicker and more resistant to the stirring and also . . . listen: the noise of the thumping of the wooden spoon will have changed a little and become deeper. Then you know the custard is cooked. I find these two clues far more reliable than the coating-of-the-back-of-the-spoon theory and so this is what I have taught Coco. As soon as the custard is cooked, remove the pan from the heat and plunge it into a sink of cold water. The difficulty is that to make good custard you should bring it as close as you dare to boiling point but not let it boil or the egg will scramble. However, if it scrambles, don't panic. Transfer it all into the blender and blast it until smooth again.

Now slice the bananas and divide them into 6 bowls or ramekins. Divide the custard between the bowls so that everybody will have more or less the same amount. Serve warm or cold with the topping of your choice.

Nigella's autumnal birthday cake

For Nigella this cake is autumnal; for us it is a spring cake simply because Coco made it for my birthday, which falls in May. She surrounded it with forget-me-nots, stuck a very appropriate, large candle in the middle and placed it in front of me, singing 'Happy Birthday'.

'Oh, *che meraviglia*,' I said. 'Where did you get it from?'

'I got it from one of my favourite books, Nigella's baking book [*How to be a Domestic Goddess*]. I was flicking through it and saw it and it looked so amazing that I thought I wanted to try it. And here it is, Nonna.'

It is indeed amazing, and, far more important, so delicious that Coco decided she wanted it for her birthday, a few days later. At the time, her mother didn't have enough maple syrup so she used maple-flavoured golden syrup instead. The cake was slightly sweeter, Coco liked it more and it was much cheaper to make.

Nigella, quite rightly, recommends eating the cake on the day it is baked.

Serves 8–10

For the cake:

175g unsalted butter, softened
100g golden caster sugar
3 organic eggs
130ml maple syrup
500g self-raising flour, sifted
175ml hot water

For the icing:

whites of 2 organic eggs
125ml maple syrup
125ml golden caster sugar
¼ tsp cream of tartar
¼ tsp sea salt
1 tsp pure vanilla extract
125g pecans, chopped

Preheat the oven to 180°C/gas mark 4. Butter and line 2 x 20cm sandwich tins with parchment paper.

Beat the butter and sugar together until pale and fluffy. Add the 3 eggs, one at a time, beating hard after each addition, and then spoon in the maple syrup. Now gradually mix in the flour, a spoonful at a time, alternating it with a little of the hot water. Beat gently until the mixture is smooth. Coco does this with an electric hand-held whisk, one of her favourite gadgets. Divide the mixture into the 2 prepared tins and bake for 40 minutes, or until a cocktail stick inserted in the middle of each cake comes out clean. Leave the cakes in their tins for 10 minutes and then unmould onto a wire rack to cool completely.

And now for the icing, which is more difficult to make than the usual royal icing since it is an Italian meringue, which is made in a bain-marie. Put everything, except the vanilla extract and the pecans, in a metal or glass bowl that fits over a pan. Put enough water in the pan to come just below the bottom of the bowl – it must not touch it. Bring the water to the boil while you beat the mixture with an electric hand-held whisk. Beat vigorously for 5–7 minutes, until the mixture forms stiff peaks, and then remove the bowl from the heat and beat in the vanilla extract.

Cut out 4 strips of parchment paper and arrange them in a square on the serving dish. These are to keep the dish clean and presentable. Put one of the cakes on the dish and spread the 'dreamy, ivory-coloured meringue' over it (as Nigella put it so perfectly). Top with the second cake and spread the remaining meringue over it and all over the sides. With a palette knife, make swirls in the icing, to create a wavy-curly look rather than a smooth one – the perfect job for any young Coco. Shower the cake all over with the pecan pieces and remember to slide out the bits of paper from under it, before you bring it triumphantly to the table.

Sweet ricotta pancakes

This is a real treat, at least for my family, although it is the sort of dish I do not make often. It takes quite a bit of time and after you finish there is a lot of clearing up – and this is something I never manage to make any of my progeny do. At the end of the cooking, they all seem to disappear.

I make the dish with Italian pancakes, which are richer than the classic English ones and, I think, provide a better complement to the ricotta stuffing; but of course you can make your usual sort. Coco often makes this with English pancakes, which she finds easier.

Serves 6–8

For the pancakes:
120g Italian 00 flour
pinch of salt
200ml semi-skimmed milk
3 organic eggs
30g unsalted butter

For the stuffing:
60g raisins
2 tbsp orange flower water
40g unsalted butter
75g soft brown sugar
500g ricotta
25g candied peel
grated rind of 1 organic lemon
½ tsp ground cinnamon
¼ tbsp ground cloves
½ tsp ground ginger
grating of nutmeg

For the sauce:
700ml full-fat milk
30g unsalted butter
30g Italian 00 flour
50g caster sugar
juice of 1 orange
yolks of 2 organic eggs

First make the batter. Sieve the flour into a bowl and add the salt and the milk in a thin stream, while beating hard with a balloon whisk. Drop in the 3 eggs one at a time, beating rapidly, and then cover the bowl with clingfilm and leave it to rest for at least half an hour.

When you are ready to make the pancakes, melt half the butter and stir it into the batter. The batter should have the consistency of thin cream. Add a couple of spoonfuls of water, if necessary. Transfer the batter into a jug, which makes the pouring later far easier.

Smear the bottom of a 15cm non-stick frying pan with a knob of the remaining butter. Put the pan on the heat until hot. Pour about 2 tablespoons of the batter into the pan, tilting it to allow the batter to run all over the bottom. Cook until the edges begin to curl and turn golden, then flip the pancake over with a fish slice and cook the other side briefly. When it is golden, transfer the pancake to a wooden board.

Take the pan off the heat between each pancake or it will become too hot and the batter will solidify before it can run over the bottom of the whole pan. Go on making pancakes in this way until you have used all the batter, adding a little more butter to the pan every now and then.

Now to the stuffing. Put the raisins in a bowl and cover with the orange flower water. Leave for 20 minutes or so. Meanwhile melt the butter and stir in the brown sugar. Push the ricotta through a food mill fitted with the disc with the smallest holes, or push it through a sieve, into a bowl. Stir in the melted butter and sugar followed by the raisins, complete with their orange flower water, the candied peel, lemon rind and all the spices. Give a spoon to your young helper to taste and correct the mixture with a little more sugar if she wants it.

Preheat the oven to 160°C/gas mark 3.

Prepare the sauce. Heat the milk to simmering point. Meanwhile in another pan, melt the butter and mix in the flour to make a roux. Cook for about 30 seconds, stirring rapidly, then remove the pan from the heat and add the milk, while stirring all the time. Put the pan back on a very low heat, mix in the sugar and cook, stirring all the time, until a few bubbles break on the surface of the sauce. Let the sauce cook for 5 minutes more, either in a bain-marie or using a heat diffuser plate. Still stir it frequently. Then allow it to cool a little before adding the orange juice and the egg yolks, one at a time, incorporating them very thoroughly.

Lightly butter a large baking dish and spread about half of the sauce over the bottom. Lay the pancakes on the work surface and spread about 1 tablespoon of the ricotta filling over each one. Roll up the pancakes – a job Coco adores – and place them, side by side, on the prepared dish. Spoon the sauce in between the pancakes and over the top and place the dish in the oven for 15 minutes. Let it rest for about 5 minutes before you serve it.

I am sure your children will love these pancakes and their pleasure will repay you for the lengthy preparation.

Brandy snaps

The other day I found Coco in her mother's kitchen armed with a palette knife, twisting something golden and sticky around the handle of a wooden spoon. 'Brandy snaps,' she declared, and I was in awe. I have never been able to make them so well. When I tried, my mixture was either too brittle and I couldn't roll it, or not cooked enough. Perhaps I didn't persevere, while Coco had, thanks to her godmother who had taught her how to make them. Coco uses maple-flavoured golden syrup, because she likes the taste. Here is the recipe given to her by her inspiring godmother.

Makes 16–18

50ml maple-flavoured
    golden syrup
40g caster sugar
50g unsalted butter
40g plain flour
½ tsp ground ginger
1 tsp brandy
whipped cream, for filling

Preheat the oven to 180°C/gas mark 4. Generously butter 2 baking trays.

Put the syrup, sugar and butter in a heavy-based saucepan and heat very gently until the sugar has dissolved and the mixture is smooth. Remove the pan from the heat and beat in the flour and ginger. Finally, add the brandy.

Drop teaspoonfuls of the mixture onto the baking trays at least 10 cm apart, because the mixture will spread in large discs during the baking, often in a rather imperfect round shape. 'It doesn't matter,' said Coco, 'because when they are rolled nobody can see it.' Bake for 8–10 minutes until each circle of mixture has become a thin, golden, lacy disc, a very attractive sight.

Take the baking trays out of the oven and let the snaps cool down for 1 minute so that they harden up a little. With a palette knife remove each disc from the baking tray and roll it around the handle of a wooden spoon. Slide the handle away and place the snap on a wire rack to cool completely. If the discs get too cold to lift and roll, put the trays back in the oven for no more than 2 minutes and try again. If your Coco has any siblings or friends around, they should all join in. Speedy shaping is the answer.

Fill the snaps with whipped cream just before serving.

Maritimers' bread

based on a recipe from the East Coast of Canada

This recipe comes in the 'Cooking for Nonna' category. Like most of my compatriots, I don't make bread by hand. I make it only in the bread machine; a loaf of white bread, with no flavouring or frills, made with an organic stoneground white flour, which I buy at my local mill shop. Actually the flour is not white at all but that grey colour which in the past was associated with poor people's bread. And how delicious it is! I make my own because I don't want any additives in my bread.

    The loaf made from this recipe is full of flavour, a bread that's best eaten on its own, generously covered with the creamy butter it deserves. It was given to Coco by Jane Mason, a Canadian friend of her mother, who has started an organisation called 'Virtuous Bread', which aims to help people find, make, and enjoy the benefits of, good bread. This is exactly how Jane wrote the recipe, which Coco dutifully followed, to produce a loaf that she proudly presented to me a few months ago.

Makes 1 loaf
160g rolled oats
175g blackstrap molasses
    (black treacle in the UK)
100g lard or butter
    (hard fat, not oil and definitely
    not margarine)
15g salt
optional: raisins. Lots of raisins.
    As many raisins as Coco
    can fit in (up to about 600g
    or you will run out of dough
    for the raisins!)
475ml boiling water

Place the oats, molasses, lard or butter, salt, and raisins if you are using them, in a big bowl and cover with the boiling water. Stir to dissolve the fat and mix everything together and leave until it is cool.

Once that is done, put 100ml warm water into a second big mixing bowl and sprinkle over the yeast. Cover, and have a cup of coffee while it proves – about 10 minutes. If it has not formed a beige sludge on the top after 10 minutes, leave it for another 10 minutes. If there is still no beige sludge, start again as the yeast is either out of date or you have killed it by using water that is too hot.

Once the yeast has proved, add the remaining warm water (300ml), the oatmeal mixture and the flour. Mix and then knead well for 10 minutes by hand or 5 minutes by machine. After a few minutes' kneading, if the dough is SUPER sticky you may need to add more flour, ½ a cup at a time. Don't be tempted to add too much flour as this dough will always be sticky – sticky is

400ml warm water (37.2 degrees
    if you want to get technical –
    that is body temperature –
    but I never measure other
    than sticking my hand in
    the water)
7g instant yeast
    or 14g active dry yeast
    or 28g fresh yeast
600g flour (any kind will
    do – I tend to use about
    400g wholewheat and 200g
    white for a bit of levity!
    You can use spelt flour too if
    you like.)

good, liquid is bad, dry is really bad. After kneading, pop it back in its bowl and let it rise until double in bulk (1–2 hours depending on the heat of the room). Squash it down and shape it with wet hands – not floured hands. This bread does well in a tin that has been well greased with either butter or lard – not oil. Fill ½–⅔ full depending on whether you have used white flour or brown flour. It also does well as a free shape (like a big ball – well, this recipe would make 2 big balls). If you bake it as balls, gently roll them in flour before popping them on a cookie sheet that you have first lined with greaseproof paper. Cover the dough and let it rise again until it has doubled in bulk (45 minutes to 1 hour).

Make some slashes in the dough (a pretty pattern is nice) and bake it in a preheated oven at 200°C/gas mark 6 for 45 minutes. The bread will sound hollow when it is done (tap the bottom to check).

It is likely this bread will be attacked by a pack of hungry people who are willing to burn their tongues as soon as it comes out of the oven. If not, let it cool before eating as this gives it a more 'together' consistency. This bread lasts well because of the fat in it and, if you are using them, because of the raisins. The oats and the fat (and the raisins) make this a 'stick to your ribs' kind of bread, perfect for a hard day at sea. Frankly I find it perfect any time anywhere.

Cheese straws

I am sure I started making these biscuits more for myself than for Coco. I was rather fed up with always making sweet biscuits and decided to teach her a savoury alternative. I *think* she liked them – frankly I cannot remember – but she certainly likes them now and it is she who makes them for me.

Makes about 30 biscuits

100g unsalted butter

150g Italian 00 flour

30g Parmigiano-Reggiano, freshly grated

½ tsp sea salt

½ tsp cayenne pepper

yolk of 1 small organic egg

Preheat the oven to 180°C/gas mark 4.

Rub the butter lightly into the flour; add the grated cheese and the seasoning. Bind the mixture with the egg yolk and knead to form a ball – you might need to add a little cold water. Roll the dough into a 3mm thick rectangle – the thinner you roll out the pastry, the better the biscuits will be, just like strands of straw, but they will also be very friable and difficult to handle without breaking. Cut the rectangle into strips about 2cm wide and 10cm long and lay these strips on a baking tray lined with parchment paper.

Bake for 12–15 minutes until just the colour of honey. Leave to cool on the tray – they are easier to handle when they are cold. Store them in a tin. Don't ask me how long you can keep them. If it is not Coco or somebody else, it is me who will finish them in one sitting.

Grissini and prosciutto

This is one of the first things Coco made when she was very young. I must admit that some of her efforts had to be remade or, more often, I took over the preparation and then gave them to her at the end to eat. She loved them. When she was young, her job was to roll the prosciutto around each grissini. Now, aged 12, she makes the grissini as well (instead of resorting to the shop-bought ones we used before). Whatever grissini you use, these snacks cannot be made much in advance, otherwise the grissini become soft.

Makes about 30 grissini

350g strong white flour
1½ tsp sea salt
3.5g fast-action dried yeast
200ml warm water
2 tbsp olive oil, plus more
    for greasing
200g prosciutto

Sieve the flour into a bowl and mix in the salt and dried yeast. Measure the warm water into a jug, add the 2 tablespoons oil and pour this into the flour, while mixing quickly to make a dough. If it seems too dry, add a little more water. Tip the dough onto the work surface and knead until smooth and elastic – this takes about 10 minutes. Transfer the dough to a lightly oiled bowl and cover the bowl with clingfilm. Put the bowl in a warm corner of the kitchen and leave for about 1 hour.

Preheat the oven to 200°C /gas mark 6. Lightly oil 2 baking trays.

Pinch off walnut-sized lumps of dough and roll them out into very thin sticks, about 15cm long. Place these sticks on the baking trays and bake for 12–15 minutes, until golden and well cooked through. Put the grissini on a wire rack to cool.

If the prosciutto slices are large, cut them in half. Roll a piece of prosciutto round one end of each grissino and arrange them, prosciutto end in the centre, on a large round dish.

(When Coco was little she also enjoyed wrapping prosciutto round some thin slices of melon (p.22), or around 4 cooked French beans, which was slightly more complicated for her small hands.)

Coco's Easter lunch

Some 2 or 3 years ago Coco announced that she was going to 'design the menu for Easter lunch and cook it all by myself'. A great offer since we were 11 for lunch, but Coco rightly thought that she could rely on 3 willing pairs of hands to help out. She knows that it is tradition in our house to have lamb for Easter preceded by hard-boiled eggs, salami and lamb's lettuce, as we do in Italy. The eggs are to celebrate the end of Lent, during which eggs were forbidden by the Catholic Church, the salami is included because it is reckoned that a salami made from the pig killed in January is just *à point* for Easter, and the lamb's lettuce is the first spring salad to be ready to eat. Ignoring the other traditional Italian Easter dish, the Colomba cake, on which she is not very keen, Coco plumped for a chocolate cake, making it fit the Easter theme by decorating it with small chocolate eggs.

So we ordered the lamb and asked the butcher to remove the bone, and we bought everything else we needed to buy, having trouble with the lamb's lettuce which here in Dorset, is practically impossible to get by itself; it's always mixed up in those bags of salad leaves, or whatever they are called. And, sadly, the lamb's lettuce in Julia's vegetable garden was not ready yet. The salami was a delicious Salame di Varzi – my favourite kind, made in Lombardy – which my son Guy had brought back from Italy, where he now lives.

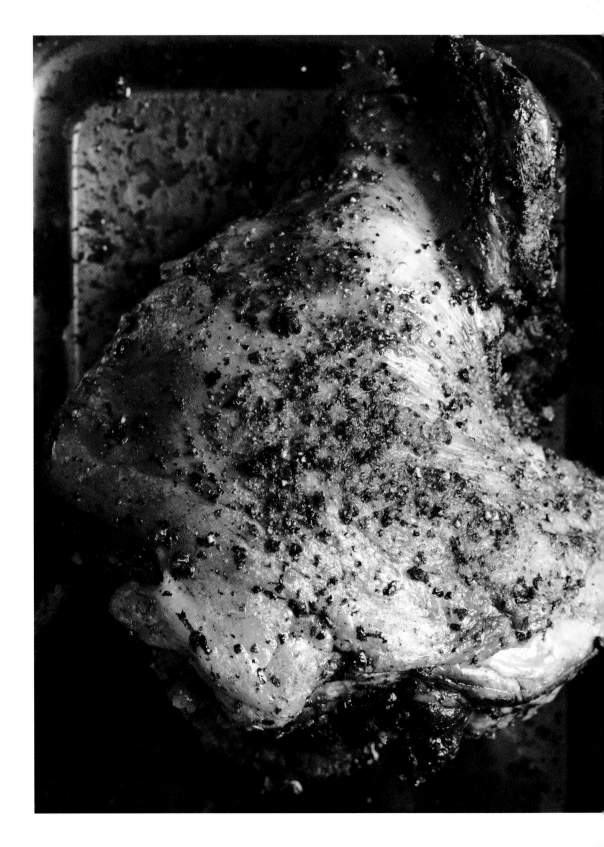

The paschal lamb

Serves 8–10

1 leg of lamb, about 2 kg,
    bone removed
2 tbsp olive oil
sea salt and freshly ground black
    pepper, to taste

For the stuffing:
3 tbsp olive oil
½ medium onion, chopped
50g fresh white breadcrumbs
    (see p.13)
150g organic dried apricots,
    chopped
25g pine nuts
1½ tsp cumin seeds
1 tbsp coriander seeds
6 peppercorns
sea salt, to taste

For the gravy:
150ml red wine
300ml meat stock

Preheat the oven to 200°C/gas mark 6.

First make the stuffing. Heat the oil in a frying pan and then add the onion. Sauté for about 7–8 minutes and then throw in the breadcrumbs and sauté everything together for a further 3 minutes, stirring very frequently. Mix in the apricots and pine nuts and sauté for some 2 minutes more, still stirring. Leave to cool slightly.

While this is going on, your helper can get the pestle and mortar out of the cupboard and start bashing the seeds and the peppercorns. Coco relishes this task, especially as she now knows how to do it properly. Empty the mortar over the frying pan, to create 'a shower of spices', add some salt and fry for another 5 minutes.

As soon as the stuffing is a bit cooler, take up a lump of stuffing and push it into the hole in the leg of lamb where the bone used to be, a most enjoyable task.

Coco left it to her father to roast the lamb, he being the family rotissier. Brush the lamb with a good tablespoon or two of olive oil and rub salt and pepper into it. Then place it on a baking dish, pour a little more oil all around and put it in the oven. After about 30 minutes turn the oven down to 150°C/gas mark 2 and leave the lamb there for another 2 hours. Take it out of the oven and put it on the side, covered with foil, and then make your gravy by pouring the meat juices into a pan, adding red wine, heating it for 2 minutes, and then adding some stock.

Our Easter lamb was perfect and Coco was applauded for her stuffing, which was indeed delicious, thanks to her excellent judgment of the amount of spices.

Chocolate cake

Makes enough to cut into
    8–10 slices
240g unsalted butter, at room
    temperature
240g caster sugar
240g self-raising flour
4 organic eggs
150g dark chocolate
    (min. 70% cocoa solids)
butter and dried breadcrumbs
    (see p.12), for the tin

Preheat the oven to 180°C/gas mark 4. Butter a 20cm springform cake tin and then sprinkle it all over with some breadcrumbs. Turn the tin upside down over the sink and tap it to let the excess crumbs fall out.

Put the butter in a bowl and mix in the sugar, beating hard to a creamy texture. Add 2 tablespoons of the flour and a little of the eggs, which your Coco has lightly beaten together. Go on adding flour and eggs until everything has gone into the bowl. Beat well.

Now for the chocolate. (Coco likes breaking it up into pieces, while she sneakily pops a small square into her mouth in spite of my protests that the quantities will be wrong if she does it too often.) Put the chocolate in a metal or heatproof glass bowl over a saucepan half-full of nearly boiling water (but make sure the water doesn't touch the bowl), and then place the saucepan on a low heat and leave it there until the chocolate has melted. Then mix it into the cake mixture. Spoon the mixture into the tin, banging the tin down to level the mixture, and put it in the oven. After about 40 minutes the cake should be cooked. Let your Coco test it with a cocktail stick, which I am sure you know should come out dry from the middle of the cake.

When the cake is done, take it out of the tin and let it cool, while you make the butter icing, on the next page, the best thing for any child to make, because of the 'licky licky' at the end.

Butter icing

125g unsalted butter, at room
   temperature
125g icing sugar, sifted
1 tsp warm water

Beat the butter really well until it is soft and then add the sugar, 1 tablespoon at a time, mixing hard with the other hand. Add the warm water and go on beating. We take it in turns to do the beating because my arm gets tired just as Coco's does. The icing is ready when it is glossy and smooth with no lumps.

When the cake is cold, spread the icing all over the top – children love doing this – and then the cake can be decorated with small chocolate eggs, chocolate chicks, chocolate bunnies or anything your Coco likes.

A Moroccan lunch

Two years ago my daughter, Julia, went to Morocco for a week. When she came back, she talked of nothing else but the food she ate there: the sardines and the *brik* (fried pastries) of Essaouira, the tagines and *b'stilla* (chicken and almond pies) of Marrakesh and the pomegranates of everywhere that actually tasted of something and not just sugared water.

Julia then bought a book, *Flavours of Morocco* by Ghillie Basan, and Coco was inspired by all the fascinating photos. Together they started cooking Moroccan food that we all enjoyed. Sometime later, Coco, with her mother's help, made this excellent lunch. We started with a lamb tagine, which she served with plenty of 'couscous studded with rubies', and then she produced a delicious mint sorbet, the perfect ending to that meaty meal.

Julia had been so captivated by the traditional mint tea, having been offered a glass at every resting point, that she devised this sorbet recipe when back home during a rare heatwave in Dorset.

Both the tagine and the couscous were not cooked in the right pots, I am afraid, but they were perfectly all right . . .

Classic lamb tagine

The recipe comes straight from Basan's book, with a minor variation. Coco does not like prunes; so she left them out and doubled the quantity of the apricots instead.

Serves 4

1–2 tbsp olive oil
2 tbsp blanched almonds
2 red onions, chopped
2–3 garlic cloves, finely chopped
5cm piece fresh ginger, peeled
    and chopped
pinch of saffron strands
2 cinnamon sticks
1–2 tsp coriander seeds, crushed
500g boned lamb from the
    shoulder or shanks, trimmed
    and cubed
12 dried apricots
3–4 strips organic orange peel
1–2 tbsp dark honey
sea salt and freshly ground
    black pepper, to taste
handful of fresh coriander
    leaves, to garnish

Heat the oil in the base of a tagine or heavy-based casserole, add the almonds and sauté until just golden. Throw in the chopped onion and garlic and cook until the onion begins to colour. Add the ginger, saffron, cinnamon sticks and coriander seeds, sauté for a minute or two and then add the meat and sauté for 2 minutes, turning it over and over so that every cube is coated in the flavouring mixture.

Pour in enough boiling water to cover and bring it to the boil. Place the lid on the pot, turn down the heat to low and simmer until the meat is tender, about 1 hour. Then throw in the apricots and orange peel strips and simmer for a further 20 minutes. After that, stir in the honey and season with salt and pepper. Continue to simmer for 10 minutes, adding, if necessary, a few tablespoons of hot water if there is not enough liquid in the pot. The liquid should be syrupy and slightly caramelised. Before you serve the dish, stir in half the fresh coriander and sprinkle the rest on the top.

Couscous studded with rubies

Coco had this idea of adding a pomegranate to the couscous one day when there was one in the house ready to be eaten. We all thought it was a brilliant idea; not only because it makes the couscous far more attractive, but also it lends a freshness that counteracts the richness of the lamb.

Serves 4

300g couscous

350ml water

6 tbsp olive oil

juice of 1 lemon

sea salt, to taste

1 or 2 ripe pomegranates

Put the couscous into a large bowl. Bring the water to the boil and pour it over. Leave the couscous to absorb the water for about 15 minutes.

Add the oil, 1 tablespoon at a time, while you mix the couscous with your hands – a job for your Coco – breaking up all the lumps with your fingertips and lifting it up to aerate it. When you have added all the oil, mix in the lemon juice and season with salt. Ask your Coco to taste and check the salt.

Now to the pomegranate, which I always find a bore to deal with. Coco is more patient than me. She taps the fruit gently all around with a wooden spoon so as to loosen all the seeds inside. Then she cuts the fruit in half and, holding each half over a bowl, she removes the seeds with her small fingers, leaving behind most of the unpleasant white pith. All the juice and seeds fall into the bowl, ready to be used. Mix the pomegranate seeds and juice into the couscous just before you are going to bring the bowl to the table.

Mint sorbet

The simplest way to prepare this sorbet is in an ice-cream maker. If you don't have an ice-cream machine, you could turn this into a granita and use the method described for the Raspberry Granita on p.116.

Serves 4–6

1 litre water

250g caster sugar

25–30 large mint leaves, plus some tiny sprigs to garnish

juice of 1 large and juicy organic lemon

Bring the water to the boil, turn off the heat and allow the water to cool for 2 minutes. This is so that the bright colour of the mint can be retained. Add the sugar, mix until dissolved and then drop in the mint leaves. Put aside to infuse for at least 5 hours.

Strain the infusion and add the lemon juice through a fine sieve. Mix well, pour the infusion into an ice-cream machine and follow the manufacturer's instructions for making a sorbet.

Serve, garnishing each bowl with a sprig of mint.

An Indian lunch

When I came back from India last year, Coco decided to give me a welcome treat. She cooked an Indian lunch and it was better than most of the food that I'd had there – of course much of the food that I ate in India was prepared in restaurants catering for tourists. But what I did eat as the Indians eat it was the fish in Goa, cooked with the utmost simplicity: grilled and dripping with garlic butter. Coco knows quite well that the fish here is seldom fresh enough to be just grilled with no frills. So she decided that a fish curry would be best, and she made this with conger eel, which happened to be on the fish stall at the market in our nearby town of Shaftesbury, but monkfish works just as well.

I first introduced Coco to eels years ago at the Rialto market in Venice and she has ever since been fascinated by this fish and its extraordinary journey. At that lunch Coco served the fish with the following curried vegetables and a big bowl of plain basmati rice, and 'piles and piles of naan', which is one of her favourite breads.

Curried vegetables

For her Indian lunch, Coco prepared this vegetable dish alongside the curried fish, see p.233. And the whole meal was delicious.

Serves 4

400g waxy potatoes
½ cauliflower head
4 tbsp groundnut or
    vegetable oil
2 onions, finely sliced
1 fresh red chilli, seeded and
    chopped
2.5cm piece fresh ginger, peeled
    and grated
2 garlic cloves, grated
1 tsp cumin seeds
1 tsp mustard seeds
400g tin chopped tomatoes
sea salt, to taste

Peel the potatoes and cut them into 2.5cm chunks. Put them in a large saucepan full of water, season with salt, bring to the boil and simmer until nearly tender. Wash the cauliflower and cut it into pieces. When the potatoes are nearly ready, add the cauliflower pieces to the pan and cook for 3 or 4 minutes, until just tender, but still very al dente. Reserve a mugful of the cooking water and then drain the vegetables.

While the vegetables are cooking, heat the oil in a large frying pan, add the onion and a pinch or two of salt and sauté for 20 minutes, turning it over frequently so that it does not catch. Then throw in the chilli, fry for 2 minutes, and then add the ginger, garlic, cumin and mustard seeds. Cook for 5 minutes, then add the tomatoes and cook for another 10 minutes. Taste and check the seasoning, then add the cooked vegetables and cook for about 20 minutes, turning them over and over in the sauce so that every piece gets well coated. You might have to add some of the reserved vegetable water during the cooking so that there is always some liquid at the bottom of the pan.

Curried fish

Serves 4

1 tsp mustard seeds

1 tsp cumin seed

3 tbsp groundnut oil

300g onions, very finely sliced

3 garlic cloves, chopped

3 green chillies, seeded
  and sliced

5cm piece fresh ginger, peeled
  and chopped

400g tin chopped tomatoes

1 tsp turmeric powder

750ml coconut milk

800g conger eel or monkfish,
  cut into 5cm chunks

sea salt, to taste

bunch of fresh coriander,
  to garnish

Put a large, heavy-based frying pan with the mustard and the cumin seeds in it on the heat until the seeds pop. Then add the oil, onion, garlic, chilli and ginger. Sprinkle straightaway with a pinch or two of salt, which prevents the onion burning, and sauté until soft but not brown – about 10 minutes – turning the mixture over every now and then.

Add the tomatoes and cook for 5 minutes and then add the turmeric and coconut milk. Season with salt and bring to the boil. Add the fish and poach for 10 minutes on a low heat. Taste and check the seasoning. Coarsely chop the coriander leaves and sprinkle over the top just before you dish it out.

Grazie

My warm *mille grazie* are for Poppy Hampson and Juliet Brooke for their endless patience in decoding and making sense of my electronically deficient manuscript, for giving it a shape and making it fit for publication. Thank you also to Will Webb, who managed to make this book look so beautiful, and to all my friends at Chatto & Windus who, in one way or another, have been involved in the production of this book.

I am very grateful to Alison Samuel who first approved of my very sketchy proposal for *Cooking with Coco*. Thank you, Alison.

A special *grazie* for Jason Lowe, who made my dream come true when he agreed to take the photographs not only of the food but also of the children.

Grazie to Vivien Green, my agent, my champion and a dear friend. She is always there to encourage me, to comment on my writing and to propel me forward with the right advice and with infectious enthusiasm.

And *grazie infinite* to another dear friend, Clare Blampied, managing director of Saclà UK, for giving me the idea of dividing the book into the four ages of Coco. And I must not forget Michelle Berriedale-Johnson, who gave me constant loving support and practical advice and suggestions. *Grazie,* Michelle and Clare.

I am also indebted to Sarah Cross, who opened her organic shop, Gold Hill, in our local village, Child Okeford, especially for the photo shoot and produced the most magnificent display of fresh fruit and vegetables.

My most heart-full thanks are for my daughter Julia, who played a big part in the making of this book. I consulted her endlessly about which recipes to include and which to leave out. She also retested a lot of recipes and wrote down invaluable comments on the children's reactions. Her name should appear on the front page.

And *grazie* to Nell and Johnny, my tasters and commentators, and to Coco, Kate, Otter and Ned, my wonderfully photogenic budding chefs.

But my loudest *grazie* is for Coco, my muse.

Lastly, and on Coco's behalf, I would like to thank her great friend Tiger Ritchie and her grandmother, for taking Coco to Paris for a cookery course two years ago. 'It was amazing what we made and ate,' Coco said.

Index

C